OLD TESTAMENT SAINTS

AND

THE MESSIAH

Jean Tankersley

Copyright © 2007 by Jean Tankersley

Old Testament Saints and The Messiah
by Jean Tankersley

Printed in the United States of America

ISBN 978-1-60477-251-7

All rights reserved solely by the author. The author guarantees all contents are original and do not infringe upon the legal rights of any other person or work. No part of this book may be reproduced in any form without the permission of the author. The views expressed in this book are not necessarily those of the publisher.

Unless otherwise indicated, Bible quotations are taken from the Authorized King James Version. New York Harper and Brothers Publishers.

www.xulonpress.com

PREFACE

Sixteen hundred years were needed to complete the writing of the Bible. It is the work of many authors who wrote by God's divine inspiration. The Bible spans almost 2000 years of history. The New Testament covers less than 100 years of history. These authors lived in different times, different places, and spoke different languages.

Scholars gathered the manuscripts written in Hebrew, Aramaic and Greek and translated them into a single language. As Peter wrote in 2 Peter 1:21, "For the prophecy came not in old time by the will of man: but Holy men of God spake as they were moved by the Holy Ghost." Paul tells us in 2 Timothy 3:16-17 "All scripture is given by inspiration of God, and is profitable for doctrine, for reproof, for correction, for instruction in righteousness: That the man of God may be perfect, thoroughly furnished unto all good works."

The Bible is a remarkable book. Millions of copies are sold each year. It has been the number one best-seller for decades. Unfortunately, the Bible is said to be the least read Book of all time.

Old Testament Saints and The Messiah is an overview of the Bible and is not a substitute. My prayer is that it will stir your imagination to a point where you will read the Word of God in it's entirety to acquaint yourself with our awesome God.

TABLE OF CONTENTS

Preface v
Chapter One - Adam and Eve 11
Two - Noah 15
Three - Abraham and Sarai 19
Four - Isaac, Rebekah, Esau and
Jacob 27
Five - Judah 37
Six - Joseph 41
Seven - Moses and Aaron 49
Eight - Joshua 67
Nine - Gideon 73
Ten - Samson 77
Eleven - Samuel and Saul 81
Twelve - David and Saul 89
Thirteen - Solomon 105
Fourteen - Elijah 111
Fifteen - Elisha 117
Sixteen - Hezekiah 123
Seventeen - Ezra 129

Eighteen - Nehemiah 135
Nineteen - Esther 141
Twenty - Job.....................................147
Twenty-One - Isaiah..........................155
Twenty-Two - Jeremiah 163
Twenty-Three - Ezekiel 169
Twenty-Four - Daniel........................173
Twenty-Five - Minor Prophets..........181
Twenty-Six - The Messiah................193
Questions for individual or group
    study session 215

DEDICATED TO MY PRECIOUS DAUGHTERS

DEBRA LYNN AND PAMELA KAY

ONE

ADAM AND EVE

When God created the heaven and the earth, He also created every type creature that swims in the water; every type of flying bird; every type of domestic and wild animal; and every type crawling creature that crawls on the earth.

God then created man in His own image. He formed Adam from the dust of the earth and breathed life into him.

He gave Adam dominion over the birds of the air, cattle and every creeping thing that creeps on the earth.

There were many fruit trees in the Garden of Eden. He put Adam in the garden to farm the land and take care of it, and allowed Adam to name each thing He had created.

The Lord wanted Adam to have a helpmate. He caused a deep sleep to come over Adam, took one of his ribs and made woman. She was called Eve. He blessed them and told them to be fruitful and multiply and fill the earth. He said, "Man shall leave his father and mother and be joined with his wife and they become one flesh."

When God put Adam and Eve in the Garden of Eden to tend it, He told them they could eat of any of the fruit, but of the tree of knowledge of good and evil, they could not eat or they would die.

They lived in fellowship with God and there was no sin in their lives. They were both naked, but were not ashamed. God blessed them and told them to be fruitful and multiply and fill the earth. They were called mankind.

The serpent was more clever than all the animals God had made. He asked Eve if the Lord told them they could eat from any tree in the garden. She told him God said they would die if they touched or ate from the forbidden tree. The serpent told her she would not die if she ate of the forbidden tree. He told her their eyes would be opened and they would be as gods and would know good and evil.

When Eve saw that the tree was good for food and would make them wise, they rebelled against God, and both of them ate of the forbidden fruit. Their eyes were opened and they knew they were naked. They sewed fig leaves together and made themselves aprons.

When God came into the garden, Adam and Eve hid from Him, as they knew they were naked. He asked them why they were hiding. They said they were naked. God asked them how they knew they were naked. Eve told God the serpent deceived her and she ate of the forbidden tree and Adam also ate from it.

The Lord had given them the opportunity for a wonderful life in the Garden of Eden, but they sinned against God and brought sin to all the world, as all have sinned.

The Lord told the serpent it would crawl on its belly and be the lowest of the animals forever. He told Eve He would increase her labor and pain when she gave birth to her children. He told Adam He would curse the ground and you shall work hard, till the ground for your food and since you were made from dust, when you die to dust you shall return.

The Lord said, "Man has now become like us and knows good and evil. Lest he puts out his hand and takes also from the tree of life and live forever, I will send him out of the garden of Eden to till the ground from which he was taken."

Adam and Eve had three sons, Cain, Abel and Seth. Cain was a farmer and Abel was a shepherd.

Abel gained God's favor when he offered a lamb to God as a sacrifice. Cain was jealous of Abel, as God had shown Abel more respect for his offering. When Cain and Abel were in the field, Cain killed Abel. God told Cain, "Because you have killed your brother, when you till the ground it will not yield its strength, and you will be a fugitive and a vagabond on this earth."

Seth was born after Cain killed Abel. The bible tells us they had other sons and daughters but does not tell their names.

Adam lived nine hundred thirty years.

TWO

NOAH

Noah was the son of Lamech. He was a descendent of Cain, and the grandson of Methuselah.

The Lord had allowed humans to live many years. When He saw all the evil in the world, He decided to only allow them to live up to one hundred twenty years.

When the Lord saw how evil humans had become on the earth, He was very sad. He told Noah He was going to wipe them from the face of the earth. He said He would also destroy all animals and birds.

Noah had three sons, Shem, Ham and Japheth. The Lord was pleased with Noah and told him to build an ark and to take his wife, his sons, their wives and a male and female of the birds, animals and creeping things into the ark to keep them alive.

Noah built the ark as the Lord had commanded him. It took Noah one hundred twenty years to build the ark. He took a male and female of every type bird, domestic animal, wild animal and creature that crawls on the earth into the ark to keep them alive. Noah took his wife, his sons and their wives onto the ark to escape the flood. The Lord told Noah to take all kinds of food for his family and the animals onto the ark. The Lord closed the door behind them. Noah was six hundred years old when the flood came.

The Lord sent rain for forty days and forty nights. The waters rose twenty-three feet above the mountain tops. The ark was lifted above the earth. The waters prevailed upon the earth one hundred fifty days. Every living person and thing on the earth died. God made a wind pass over the earth and the waters receded. After the waters receded, and the earth dried, Noah, his family, the birds, animals and creeping things came out of the ark. Noah built an altar and sacrificed to the Lord..

God made a covenant with Noah, his sons and all seed after them, that He would never again curse the ground for mans sake, nor would He ever again smite every thing living. He would never bring a flood to destroy the earth. He told them He would put a rainbow in the clouds to remind Him of the everlasting covenant between Him and every living creature of all flesh that is on the earth. While the earth remains, seedtime, harvest, cold, heat, winter, summer, day and night shall not cease.

He blessed them and told Noah, Shem, Ham and Japheth to be fruitful, multiply and replenish the earth. All the animals, fish, birds and creatures that crawl on the ground have been put under your control.

Noah, a farmer, was the first person to plant a vineyard. He drank the wine, got drunk, and lay naked. His son, Ham, who was the father of Canaan, saw him naked and told his two brothers. His brothers took a garment, walked backwards, and covered their father. When Noah sobered up and found what Ham had done, He cursed Ham's son, Canaan, and said he would be a servant of his brothers. He blessed Shem and Japheth and said Canaan will be their servant.

Shem had twenty-six descendents; Ham had thirty descendents; and Japheth had fourteen descendents. These are the families whereby the nations divided in the earth after the flood. However, all of

Canaan. At that time the Canaanites were in the land. The Lord told Abraham, "Look from the place you are standing, north, south, east and west. The land you see I give to you and your descendents forever. I will make your descendents as numerous as the dust of the earth. You shall be the father of many nations." Abraham built an altar to the Lord.

Abraham then went to Bethel and Negev.

There was a famine in the land and Abraham went to Egypt. He told his wife, Sarah, to tell everyone she was his sister. He was afraid the Egyptians would kill him and take Sarah, as she was very beautiful. Pharaoh took Sarah to his palace. The Lord sent plagues to Pharaoh and his house because he had taken Sarah. Pharaoh asked Abraham, "Why did you say Sarah was your sister and not your wife?" Abraham told Pharaoh he was afraid the Egyptians would kill him and take Sarah. Pharaoh was very angry. He sent Abraham and Sarah away.

Abraham was very rich because he had livestock, silver and gold. Lot, who had been traveling with him, also had his own sheep, cattle and tents. There was not enough pasture land for both of them. They decided to separate and Lot took the whole Jordan plain. Abraham lived in Canaan.

Everything went well for Abraham. He was given sheep, cattle, donkeys, camels and slaves. He traveled to the land of Canaan. The Lord told him to look in all directions and the land he saw, the Lord was giving it to Abraham and to his seed forever. He said count the stars if you can, and that is how many descendents you will have.

The Lord made a deep sleep come over Abraham. He told Abraham, "Your descendents will live in a land that is not theirs and they will serve and be afflicted by them four hundred years. However, the nation they serve, I will judge, and they will come out with great possessions. After that they shall come out and serve Me in this place."

Sarah was barren and had no children. She told Hagar, her Egyptian handmaid, to go in and lay with Abraham so she could have children by her. After Hagar conceived, she began despising Sarah. Sarah dealt harshly with her and Hagar ran away. The Angel of the Lord found her and told her to go back to Sarah, as she was going to have a son and should name him Ishmael. The Lord said Ishmael will be the father of twelve princes and I will make him a great nation.

Old Testament Saints and The Messiah

When Abraham was ninety-nine years old, the Lord spoke to him and told him Sarah would have a son and they would name him Isaac. God made a covenant with Abraham and told him he would be the father of many nations and Sarah would be a mother of nations and kings would be of her. The Lord also gave Abraham and his descendents the land of Canaan.

The Lord did as He had promised and Sarah had a son. Abraham was one hundred years old and Sarah was ninety years old when Isaac was born. The Lord told Abraham, "My covenant I will establish for Isaac."

Sodom and Gommorah, where Lot and his family lived, was so evil that God said He would destroy it. He told Lot and his family to flee and not look back. Lot's wife looked back and turned into a pillar of salt. Lot and his two daughters fled to Zoar. They later settled in the mountains and lived in a cave.

As Abraham traveled to Gerar, he again told Sarah to say she was his sister. Abimelech took Sarah into his house, but the Lord came to Abimelech in a dream and told him Sarah was a man's wife. The Lord had closed all the wombs of the house of Abimelech. Abimelech was angry with Abraham. Abraham prayed for Abimelech and Abimelech's wife and all his maidservants could again bear children.

Abimelech gave Abraham silver, sheep and oxen and let Abraham and Sarah live in his land.

After Isaac was born, Abraham gave a huge feast. Sarah saw the son of Hagar laughing at Isaac. Sarah told Abraham to send Hagar and her son away, as he should never share the inheritance with her son Isaac. Abraham was upset, as this was also his son. He told Sarah to do as she wished and she sent Hagar and Ishmael away. God told Abraham not to grieve, as He would make Ishmael a great nation, and through Isaac your descendents will carry your name.

Abraham gave Hagar bread and water and sent her and her son away. They wandered around in the desert. When the water was gone, she placed her son under a bush. She went a short way from him and began to sob. She was sure he was going to die and she did not want to see him die. God heard the boy crying and sent His angel to see why the boy was crying. God opened Hagar's eyes and she saw a well. She filled her container and gave her son a drink. God told Hagar He was going to make her son into a great nation. When Ishmael grew up, he lived in the desert and became a skilled archer.

God tested Abraham's faith and told him to take Isaac to Moriah and offer him as a burnt offering on one of the mountains which I shall show you. Abraham took the child, as God had instructed. He built an altar and placed the wood on the altar. He then took his son, bound him and laid him on the wood on the altar. He drew back his knife to slay his son when an angel of the Lord called to him, saying, "Do not harm the boy." God told Abraham He would bless him and would multiply his seed as the stars of the heaven and the sand on the seashore, because Abraham had obeyed His voice.

Sarah lived one hundred twenty-seven years and then died. Abraham purchased a tomb where she could be buried.

Abraham took another wife. Her name was Keturah. She bore him six sons. Abraham gave all his sons gifts and sent them away from his son Isaac.

When Abraham was old, he told his senior servant of his household to promise him he would not get Isaac a wife from the Canaanites. He told him to go to the land of his relatives and get a wife for Isaac there. The servant did as Abraham requested. He got Isaac a wife, who was the daughter of Bethuel, son of Milcah, who was the wife of Abraham's brother, Nahor.

Abraham lived one hundred seventy-five years. When he died, he gave Isaac all he had.

FOUR

ISAAC, REBEKAH, ESAU AND JACOB

Isaac was the son of Abraham and Sarah. Esau and Jacob were the twin sons of Isaac and Rebekah.

When Abraham was old, he told his servant, Eliezer, to go to the land of his family to find a wife for his son Isaac.

Abraham did not want his son to take a wife of the daughters of the Canaanites. The servant did as Abraham directed. He traveled to Aram Naharaim where Nahor, Abraham's brother, lived.

The women came to the well in the evening to draw water. The servant rested by the well and prayed for the Lord to send him the right woman for Isaac. Before he finished praying, Rebekah came to the well with her jug to get water. The servant asked her

Old Testament Saints and The Messiah

---

for a drink of water. She gave it to him and also drew water for his camels to drink. She was the daughter of Nahor's son, Bethuel. Laban, Rebekah's brother, asked the servant to spend the night.

The servant told Laban that Abraham had sent him to find a wife for his son, Isaac. He told them how wealthy Abraham was and that he was going to leave everything to Isaac. Laban and Bethuel agreed to let Rebekah go and she became Isaac's wife. Isaac was forty years old when he took Rebekah as his wife.

Rebekah was barren and Isaac prayed to God that Rebekah would bear him a son. Rebekah conceived and had twin boys. Their names were Esau and Jacob.

As the boys grew, Esau was a skillful hunter and a man of the field. Jacob was a plain man, dwelling in tents.

One day Jacob prepared a stew. When Esau came in from the field, he was very tired. He asked Jacob to give him some of the stew. Jacob said, "If you will sell me your birthright I will give you some stew." Esau sold Jacob his birthright for a bowl of stew.

The Lord told Isaac not to go to Egypt but live in the land He would show him. The Lord said He would bless Isaac and make his descendents multiply as the stars of heaven. The Lord said, "I will give to your descendents all these lands and in your seed all nations will be blessed because Abraham kept My commandments."

There was a famine in the land and Isaac went to Abimelech, king of the Philistines in Gerar.

When the men asked Isaac about his wife, he told them she was his sister, as she was very lovely and he was afraid they would kill him and take her.

After Isaac and Rebekah had been there a long time, Abimelech saw them embracing. Abimelech called Isaac and asked why he said Rebekah was his sister and not his wife. Isaac told him he was afraid he would be killed because of her.

Abimelech allowed them to stay in his land. Isaac sowed the land and became very rich. God blessed him and he had flocks, herds and a great store of servants. The Philistines envied him and they filled all the wells Abraham's servants had dug. Finally, Abimelech sent Isaac and Rebekah away, as Isaac had become more powerful than them.

They went to Beersheba. The Lord appeared to Isaac and told him He would bless him and multiply

Old Testament Saints and The Messiah

his seed for his servant Abraham's sake. Isaac built an altar there and worshipped the Lord.

When Isaac was old and could hardly see, he called his older son Esau to him and said, "Go to the field and get some venison and make me savory meat which I love and bring it to me that I may bless you before I die."

Isaac loved Esau more, but Rebekah loved Jacob more. Rebekah overheard what Isaac had said to Esau, and she called her son Jacob. She told him to bring meat so she could make Isaac savory meat and Jacob could take it to his father to receive the blessing. She put Esau's clothes on Jacob and skins from the goat on Jacob's hands and neck, as Esau was a hairy man.

Jacob took the meat, bread and wine to his father. He told Isaac he was his son Esau. Isaac blessed Jacob, saying, "May God give you the dew of heaven and the fatness of the earth and plenty of grain and wine. People will serve you and nations bow down to you. You will be master over your brethren."

Jacob left the room. When Esau came into the room to bring his father's meat, he found Jacob had been there, deceived his father and received his blessing. Esau was very angry, so Isaac blessed him and told him, "Your dwelling will be the fatness of the earth and the dew of the heavens above. I have made Jacob your lord and given him all his brothers as servants. You will live by the sword and serve your brother, but eventually you shall receive your freedom."

Esau swore he would kill Jacob. Rebekah was told the words of her son Esau. She called Jacob, told him to flee and go to Paddan Aram to her brother. Isaac also told Jacob not to take a wife from the daughters of Canaan.

Isaac was one hundred eighty years old when he died.

Jacob left Beersheba and traveled toward Haran. When it was late in the evening, he stopped to sleep. He had a dream that he saw a ladder reaching to heaven and angels going up and down the ladder. He saw the Lord standing above it. The Lord said to him, "I am giving this land, on which you are lying, to you and your descendents. Your descendents shall be many and you shall spread abroad to the east, west, north and south. In you and your seed all the families of the earth will be blessed. Jacob took the rock which was under his head and made it a marker.

The next day Jacob traveled on to Haran. Rachel, the daughter of Laban, came to the well where Jacob was, to water her father's sheep. He told Rachel he was Rebekah's son. When Laban heard this, he took Jacob into his home.

After Jacob had stayed with Laban one month, he told Laban he would work for him seven years if he would give him his youngest daughter, Rachel, to marry. After the seven years were complete, Jacob asked Laban for Rachel. Laban gave a wedding feast and later that evening, Laban took Leah in to Jacob to sleep with her. When morning came, Jacob realized he was sleeping with Leah and not Rachel. Jacob asked Laban why he had tricked him. Laban said it was their tradition that the oldest daughter marry first.

Jacob worked another seven years for Laban's daughter Rachel.

Jacob loved Rachel more than Leah and God saw this. He made it possible for Leah to have children.

Rachel was barren, but Leah bore Jacob six sons and one daughter, Reuben, Simeon, Levi, Judah, Issachar, Zebulun and Dinah.

Rachel was angry, so she sent Bilhah, her maid, in to Jacob so she would bear a son for Rachel. Bilhah conceived and had a son. She named him Dan. She had another son and named him Naphtali.

When Leah saw that she had stopped bearing, she sent her maid, Zilpah, in to Jacob. She bore Jacob two sons, Gad and Asher.

God remembered Rachel and opened her womb. She bore Jacob a son and named him Joseph.

Laban's countenance turned against Jacob, as Jacob had become very rich. The Lord said unto Jacob, "Return unto the land of thy fathers and to thy kindred; and I will be with thee." (Genesis 31:3) Jacob fled with his wives, children and all he had.

Jacob was alone one night and wrestled with a Man until dawn. The Man prevailed not against him. He touched the hollow of Jacob's thigh and the hollow of Jacob's thigh was out of joint. The Man told Jacob to let him go. Jacob would not let him go until he had blessed him. The Man changed Jacob's name to Israel. Jacob said, "I have seen God face to face and my life is preserved." (Genesis 32:30)

Esau married Adah, the daughter of Elon, the Hittite, Aholibamah, the daughter of Anah and Bashemath, Ishmael's daughter. Esau settled in the area around Mt. Seir and became very rich. Jacob did not know this. When Jacob looked and saw Esau at a distance, he separated his wives and children and all he had into groups so all would not be killed by Esau. If Esau and his men attacked one group, the others could run away.

Jacob sent his messengers to tell Esau he was coming with all his oxen, flocks, womanservants and menservants. Tell him I have sent my messengers to tell him I wish to find grace in his sight. The messengers returned and told Jacob his brother Esau was coming to meet him with four hundred men. Jacob was afraid and he asked the Lord to deliver him from the hand of his brother Esau. Jacob sent before him goats, ewes, rams, camels and bulls to be given to Esau as a present.

When Esau and his four hundred men arrived, Esau ran to meet Jacob, embraced and kissed him, and they wept. Esau did not want to take the present Jacob had offered him, but Jacob insisted. Esau returned to Mt. Seir and founded the nation of Edom and Jacob journeyed to Succoth.

Jacob's daughter, Dinah, was raped by Shechem, the son of Hamar the Hivite, prince of the country. Shechem loved Dinah and wanted to marry her. However, her brothers, Simeon and Levi, were very angry because he had defiled their sister. They slew

Shechem, Hamar and all the men of the city. Simeon and Levi took all their sheep, oxen, donkey's and all their wealth, their little ones and their wives.

God changed Jacob's name to Israel and told him to go to Bethel and dwell there. God said unto him, "I am God Almighty; be fruitful and multiply; a nation and a company of nations shall be of thee, and kings shall come out of thy loins; and the land which I gave to Abraham and Isaac, to thee I will give it, and to thy seed after thee I will give the land." (Genesis 35:11-12)

Rachel died giving birth to a son, Benjamin. She was buried in Bethlehem.

The sons of Jacob were twelve: The sons of Leah were Reuben, Simeon, Levi, Judah, Issachar and Zebulun; the sons of Rachel were Joseph and Benjamin; the sons of Bilhah were Dan and Naphtali; the sons of Zilpah were Gad and Asher.

Esau took his wives, children and all he had and went to another land away from his brother Jacob. They had too many possessions to live together, as there was not enough pasture land for their livestock.

The sons and generations of Esau were dukes and kings. Esau was the father of the people of Edom.

Judah went to visit an Adullamite named Hirah. There he saw a daughter of a Canaanite whose name was Shua. He married her.

They had a son and named him Er. He was wicked in the site of the Lord, and the Lord killed him.

The sons of Judah were Er, Onan, Shelah, Perez and Zerah.

Before Judah's father died, he called his sons together to tell them what would happen to each of them.

He told Judah, "Your brothers shall praise you. The scepter shall not depart from Judah, nor a lawgiver from between his feet, until Shiloh comes, and to Him shall be the obedience of the people."

After the death of Joshua, the children of Israel asked the Lord who would go up against the Canaanites to fight against them? The Lord said, "Judah shall go up, as I have delivered the land into his hand." Judah took his brother, Simeon, to fight with him against the Canaanites.

The Lord became very angry with Israel and removed them from His sight; there was none left but the tribe of Judah.

Judah failed to keep the Lord's commandments and walked in the statutes Israel had made. The Lord rejected all the descendents of Israel, afflicted them, delivered them into the hands of plunderers and removed them from His sight.

The Lord said, "There is a day coming when I will make a new covenant with the house of Israel and the house of Judah. I will put My law in their minds and write it on their hearts. I will be their God and they shall be My people."

SIX

JOSEPH

⚜

Joseph was the son of Rebekah and Jacob (whose name God changed to Israel). Israel loved Joseph more than any of his sons, as he was the son of his old age. He made Joseph a coat of many colors. Joseph's brothers envied him because his father loved him more. In Joseph's dreams, his brothers were always bowing down to him, so they hated him for his dreams.

The brother's were feeding the flock at Shechem and from there they went to Dothan. Israel told Joseph to go check on his brothers and the flock and see if all was well. When the brothers saw him coming, they said to one another, "Let us slay him, and cast him into a pit and we will tell our father a wild beast devoured him."

Reuben told his brothers, "Do not kill him, but cast him in a pit." Reuben wanted to come back later and take Joseph from the pit and return him to his father. The other brothers took his coat of many colors and cast him into the pit. As they were eating, a group of Ishmeelites came from Gilead. They said, "Let's sell him to the Ishmeelites." They drew him up out of the pit and sold him for twenty pieces of silver. The Ishmeelites took Joseph to Egypt.

When Reuben returned to get Joseph, he was not there. Reuben tore his clothes and was very depressed.

His brother's killed a goat and dipped Joseph's coat in the blood. They took it to their father and told him beasts must have devoured Joseph. His father mourned for his son for many days and could not be comforted.

Joseph was sold to Potiphar, an officer of Pharaoh and captain of the guard. The Lord was with Joseph and he was a prosperous man. He found grace in the sight of Pharaoh, as Pharaoh could see that the Lord was with Joseph in all he did. Pharaoh made him overseer over all of his house. The Lord blessed the Egyptian's house for Joseph's sake; and the blessing of the Lord was on all he had in the house and in the field.

Pharaoh's wife wanted Joseph to lay with her. He told her he would not do such a wicked thing and sin against God. When he continued to refuse, she told everyone he came in to lie with her and she cried with a loud voice. When Pharaoh heard this, he put Joseph in prison. The Lord was with Joseph and showed him mercy and gave him favor in the sight of the keeper of the prison.

The kings cupbearer and baker offended the king. He put them in prison where Joseph was, and the captain of the guard assigned them to Joseph.

After they had been there quite some time, they both had dreams. The next morning Joseph asked them why they looked so unhappy. They both said they had disturbing dreams and there was no one to interpret them. Joseph told them only God could interpret them. He asked the cupbearer what his dream was. Joseph interpreted it for him and the cupbearer was very pleased. Joseph told him to remember him when things were going good for him and get him out of prison. Joseph interpreted the baker's dream, however, it was not a good dream as Joseph said the dream shows he would die soon. The cupbearer's dream came true, but he did not remember Joseph.

Two years later, Pharaoh had a dream and called for all the magicians of Egypt and the wise men. None of these could interpret Pharaoh's dream. The butler remembered Joseph had interpreted his dream when he was in prison and he told Pharaoh.

Pharaoh called for Joseph, told him his dream and asked Joseph to interpret it. Joseph said, "It is not me, God shall give Pharaoh an answer of peace." (Genesis 41:16). Joseph told Pharaoh his dream meant there would be seven years of plenty in Egypt and would be followed by seven years of famine. He told Pharaoh he should appoint men, discreet and wise, and set them over the land of Egypt. Appoint officers over the land to take a fifth part in the seven years of plenty and store it for the seven years of famine.

Pharaoh was pleased with Joseph and knew the Spirit of God was in Joseph. He put Joseph over his house and allowed him to rule the people of Egypt. He gave Joseph a wife, Asenath, the daughter of Potipherah, the priest of On. She bore Joseph two sons, Manasseh and Ephraim.

Joseph went throughout all the land of Egypt. The seven plentiful years brought forth abundantly.

Joseph gathered food during this seven years of plenty and laid up the food in the cities to have food for the next seven years.

The seven years of plenty ended, however, Joseph had laid in store enough food to last through the seven years of famine. All the land of Egypt was famished and the people cried to Pharaoh for bread. He told the people to go to Joseph who opened all the store houses and sold to the Egyptians. Everyone came to Joseph for grain as the famine was severe all over the world.

When Jacob saw there was corn in Egypt, he sent his sons to Egypt to buy corn. He did not send his youngest son, Benjamin, for fear something might happen to him. As soon as Joseph saw his brothers, he recognized them. They did not recognize Joseph. Joseph accused them of being spies in order to see his younger brother, Benjamin. He kept Simeon in prison while the other brothers took corn to their family. Joseph told them to bring the other brother when they returned or they would not see his face again.

The brothers went home and told their father what Joseph had said. Jacob refused to let Benjamin go. However, when their food ran out he changed his mind and allowed all of them to go to Joseph for more corn. He sent gifts to Joseph. Joseph asked the brothers to have bread with him. Joseph was overcome when he saw Benjamin and found his father was alive and in good health. He entered into his chamber and wept. He washed his face and went back to have bread with his brothers.

Joseph filled all their sacks with food for the famine of their households. He also put his cup in Benjamin's sack and told his servant to follow them and find the cup and bring all of them back to him. Judah begged Joseph to keep him as a servant and let Benjamin return to their father with his brothers.

Joseph could no longer hide his emotions. He ordered everyone to leave the room except his brothers. Joseph told the brothers he was Joseph whom they had sold into Egypt. He told them not to be grieved, for God sent me before you to preserve life. "You did not send me hither, but God; and He hath made me a father to Pharaoh, and lord of all his house and a ruler throughout all the land of Egypt." (Genesis 45:8)

Go tell my father I am lord of Egypt and tell him to come to me. He can bring his children, grandchildren, flocks and herds and everything he has and I will let him live in the land of Goshen. Joseph kissed all his brothers and sent wagons, food and clothing with his brothers to bring his father to him.

When the brothers told Jacob his son, Joseph, was alive, and governor over all the land of Egypt, he did not believe them. When he saw the wagons, he knew Joseph had sent for him and all the families of his brothers. God spoke to Jacob and said, "Fear not to go down into Egypt, for I will there make of thee a great nation." (Genesis 46:3)

Joseph placed his father and brethren in Rameses, the best of the land of Egypt. He also furnished them with food according to the number of children they had.

The famine was so bad in Egypt that the people ran out of money. They came to Joseph and told him they had no money to buy grain.. He told them to bring livestock and he would give them grain.

The next year the people came to Joseph and told him they had no money and no more livestock. He told them he would give them grain for their land. Joseph bought all the land in Egypt for Pharaoh. He gave the people seed and told them when they harvested their crops to give one-fifth of the produce to Pharaoh.

Joseph's father, Jacob, made Joseph promise not to bury him in Egypt. He wanted to be buried with his ancestors. Joseph made the promise.

When the time grew nigh for Jacob to die, he called Joseph to bring his sons for him to bless. Joseph took his sons, Manasseh and Ephraim, to Jacob. Joseph was upset when his father put his right hand on Ephraim, the youngest son. Jacob said, "Both sons will be great, but Ephraim will be greater and his seed shall become a multitude of nations."

When Jacob died, Joseph and all his brothers took him back to Canaan and buried him.

Joseph dwelt in Egypt, he and his father's house. He told his brethren, "I am about to die and God will surely visit you, and bring you out of this land unto the land which he sware to Abraham, to Isaac and to Jacob." (Genesis 50:24)

Joseph lived one hundred ten years.

SEVEN

MOSES AND AARON

⚜

Moses and Aaron were the sons of Amram and Jochebed. Moses was the first and greatest Prophet.

The children of Israel who came to Egypt, each with his own household, were Reuben, Simeon, Levi, Judah, Issacher, Zebulun, Benjamin, Dan, Naphtali, Gad and Asher. These were all descendents of Jacob. Joseph was already in Egypt.

Joseph, all his brothers and that generation died, but the children of Israel were fruitful and increased abundantly and the land was filled with them.

A new king came to Egypt who did not know Joseph. He told his people, "The children of Israel are more and mightier than we and we must deal with them lest they multiply, and in the event of war they join our enemies and fight against us."

He increased the labor and made the children of Israel work very hard, but the more he afflicted them, the more they multiplied and grew.

Pharaoh told the midwives to kill all the boy babies born to the Hebrew women, but to save the girl babies. The midwives feared the Lord and did not kill the boy babies. When confronted by Pharaoh, the midwives told him the Hebrew women were lively and delivered before they could get to them.

Pharaoh then told his people that every son born to the Hebrew women were to be cast into the river.

When Moses was born to Amram and Jochebed, they saw what a beautiful child he was and his mother hid him for three months.

When she could no longer hide him, she built an ark, placed him in it and put it among the flags by the river bank. His sister, Miriam, hid to see what would happen to him. Pharaoh's daughter came down to the river to bathe. Her maidens were walking along the river bank and found the ark with Moses in it. Pharaoh's daughter immediately realized this was one of the Hebrew' children. Miriam ran up to them and asked if they would like for her to take the baby to a Hebrew woman to nurse. She told Miriam yes, and Miriam took the baby to his mother. The child grew and the mother took him to Pharaoh's daughter and he became her son. She named him Moses.

When Moses was grown, he went out to see his brethren and their burdens. He saw an Egyptian beating a Hebrew. He killed the Egyptian and buried him in the sand. The next day he went out and saw two Hebrew men fighting. When he asked why they were fighting, they rebuked him and told him they saw him kill the Egyptian the day before.

Moses was afraid Pharaoh would hear of this and want to kill him, so he fled from Pharaoh and went to the priest of Midian.

Moses was sitting by a well one day when seven daughters of the priest of Midian came to water their father's sheep. Some shepherds came and ran them away. When Moses saw this, he came to their rescue and watered their sheep. When they arrived home, their father asked why they were home so early. They told him an Egyptian rescued them from some shepherds and drew water for the sheep. He told his daughters to go invite Moses to supper.

The priest gave Moses his daughter, Zipporah. She bore him a son and they called him Gershom.

The king of Egypt died and the children of Israel complained about their bondage. God heard their cry and remembered His covenant with Abraham, Isaac and Jacob.

While Moses was tending the flock for his father-in-law, he led the flock to Horeb, the mountain of God. The angel of the Lord appeared to Moses in a burning bush. The bush was on fire but it was not burnt. He told Moses He had seen the affliction of His people and He would bring them up out of Egypt and lead them to a land flowing with milk and honey.

God told Moses, "Gather all the elders of Israel and tell them God has seen their affliction and He will bring them up out of Egypt. Then go to the king of Egypt and ask him to let you go three days into the wilderness to sacrifice to the Lord." Moses told the Lord he was too slow of speech to talk with the king. The Lord sent Moses brother, Aaron, with him.

Moses went to his father-in-law and asked permission to return to Egypt to check on his brothers. Jethro told Moses to go in peace. Moses took his wife and sons and returned to Egypt.

Many times Moses and Aaron went to the king and asked to go for three days to sacrifice to the Lord and each time he refused. God sent many plagues on

Old Testament Saints and The Messiah

the Egyptians to show them He was God and there was no other like Him in all the world. The king still refused to let them go. He had the slave drivers increase the Israelites work. The people then blamed Moses for their mistreatment. They said Moses made Pharaoh and his officials hate them.

Moses asked the Lord why He was allowing the Egyptians to treat His people so cruelly.

The Lord told Moses to tell the Israelites, "I will bring you out of this slavery and take you to the land I promised Abraham, Isaac and Jacob." Moses told this to the Israelites, but they did not believe him because they were so discouraged by their hard work.

After God had sent many plagues on the Egyptians, Pharaoh still refused to let them go.

The Lord told Moses He would bring one more plague on Pharaoh and the Egyptians and then he will let the people go. When he does, he will force all of you to leave. At this time, tell the people of Israel that each man and woman must ask the Egyptians for silver and gold jewelry.

The Lord made the Egyptians kind to the people. Moses was highly respected by Pharaoh's officials and all Egyptians.

Finally the Lord told Moses, "Tell the king I will go out about midnight in the midst of Egypt and all the firstborn children and beasts shall die."

The Lord hardened Pharaoh's heart and he would not let the children of Israel go out of his land.

The Lord spoke to Moses and Aaron and said, "In ten days tell all the congregation of Israel to take a lamb for each household and on the fourteenth day they shall kill the lamb in the evening. Take the blood and put it on the two side posts and upper door posts of your houses. Roast the lamb and eat it and do not leave your houses until morning. I will pass through Egypt this night and smite all the firstborn, both man and beast, in the land of Egypt. When I see the blood, I will pass over you and you will not be harmed."

The Lord gave them instructions of the ordinance of the Passover. He told the children of Israel to keep the ordinance from year to year and to tell their children, "This is done because on this day the Lord brought the children of Israel out of Egypt."

At midnight the Lord struck all the first born children and all the firstborn of the livestock. There was great sadness in all of Egypt as there was not a house without one dead. Pharaoh called for Moses and Aaron during the night and told them to take all the children of Israel, their flocks and herds, leave Egypt and go serve the Lord as they wished.

About six hundred thousand men, plus the women and children of Israel, traveled from Rameses to Succoth. The children of Israel had been in Egypt four hundred thirty years when Pharaoh finally let them go.

The angel of God who went before the camp of Israel, moved and went behind them. The pillar of the cloud went before them and stood behind them. It came between the camp of the Egyptian's and the camp of Israel.

The Lord hardened Pharaoh's heart again and Pharaoh said, "Why have we let Israel go from serving us?" Pharaoh took all his chariots, army and captains and followed the children of Israel.

The children of Israel complained to Moses that they would have been better off to have stayed in Egypt rather than be killed in the wilderness.

Moses told the children of Israel to trust God and He would save them. Moses took the rod, stretched out his hand over the sea and the Lord caused the water to part. The children of Israel walked across on dry ground.

The Egyptian's pursued and went after them into the midst of the sea, with Pharaoh's horses, army and horsemen. God told Moses to stretch out his hand over the waters. The waters returned and covered all of Pharaoh's army, men, horses and chariots and they all perished in the sea. The children of Israel saw what the Lord had done for them and they feared and believed the Lord and his servant Moses.

Moses brought the children of Israel from the Red Sea into the wilderness of Shur. For three days they did not find water. They again complained to Moses. Moses prayed for the Lord to give them water. When they came to Marah the water was bitter and they could not drink it. The Lord showed Moses a tree and when it was cast into the waters they were made sweet.

The people began to complain they did not have bread. They were wishing they had not left Egypt, as they had plenty of food while in Egypt. The Lord told Moses He would rain bread from heaven for them. The children of Israel ate manna for forty years until they came to the border of Canaan.

The children of Israel then complained because they had no meat to eat. The Lord sent quail and they lay in heaps on the ground.

Old Testament Saints and The Messiah

The children of Israel traveled to Rephidim and there was no water. The Lord said to Moses, "Take the elders and the rod you smote the river with and I will stand before you. Hit the rock with the rod and water will come out."

Jethro, Moses father-in-law, saw Moses judging the people from morning to evening. He told Moses he should choose able men of Israel to help him judge the people of Israel.

Moses did as his father-in-law suggested and chose able men out of Israel to help him judge the people. The hard cases were sent to Moses to judge and the smaller matters were judged by the men Moses chose.

The children of Israel then traveled to the desert of Sanai. The Lord spoke to Moses, "Lo, I come unto thee in a thick cloud, that the people may hear when I speak with thee, and believe thee forever." (Exodus 19:9) On the third day, in the morning, there were thunders and lightnings and a thick cloud on the mount. The voice of the trumpet was very loud. All the people in the camp trembled. The Lord spoke to the children of Israel, giving them the Ten Commandments, the judgments, laws concerning violence, thefts and trespasses, moral and religious

Sabbaths and feasts. The people answered and said, "All the words which the Lord has said, we will do."

The Lord then called Moses up to the mount. He gave Moses instructions on how to build the Tabernacle, the Ark, and the mercy seat. He also explained the ceremonies of consecrating the priests. When the Lord finished instructing Moses, He gave him two tables of testimony, tables of stone, written with the finger of God. Moses was on the mount with God forty days and forty nights.

When Moses did not return, the people asked Aaron to make them gods to go before them. Aaron took all the golden earrings and made them a golden calf. When the Lord saw what Aaron had done, He sent Moses back to the people as they were worshipping the molten calf and offered sacrifices to it. The people said this was the god who brought them out of Egypt.

The Lord was so angry with the people, He told Moses He was going to destroy them. Moses pleaded with the Lord not to do this. The Lord reconsidered his threat to destroy the people.

When Moses saw the people dancing and saw the calf, he became very angry. He cast the tables out of his hands and broke them beneath the mount. He then took the calf, burned it, ground it to powder, put it in the water and made the children of Israel drink it.

Moses said, "Who is on the Lord's side?" All the sons of Levi gathered around him. He told them to go throughout the camp and slay every man. About three thousand men were slain that day. The Lord said He would blot out of His book every one who sinned against Him.

The Lord told Moses to hew two tables of stone, bring them up to the mount, and He would write the words that were in the first tables which Moses had broken.

The children of Israel left Mt. Sanai and traveled to Paran. They continued to complain and it displeased the Lord. The Lord burned among them and some were consumed. When Moses prayed to the Lord, the fire was quenched.

When the children of Israel continued to complain that they did not have meat to eat, the Lord said, "I will furnish meat and you shall eat it one whole month, until it comes out your nostrils and it will be loathsome to you." The Lord sent quails and there were many on the face of the earth. The people gathered them and as they ate, the wrath of the Lord was kindled against them and the Lord smote them with a very great plague. There they buried the people who lusted.

Aaron and his sister, Miriam, began to criticize Moses because he was married to a woman from Sudan. The Lord heard their complaint. He told Aaron and Miriam that Moses was the most faithful person in His household. He told them they should have been afraid to criticize His servant Moses. The Lord caused Miriam to be covered with an infectious disease. She was put outside the camp for seven days.

God spoke to Moses and said, "Send one man from each tribe to check on the land of Canaan which I am giving them. See if the land is good and what the people are like and return with their answers."

The men explored the land. They were gone for forty days, and when they returned, they said the land surely flowed with milk and honey. They said the people who live there are strong and some are giants.

Joshua and Caleb wanted to go at once and possess it, as they knew the Lord was with them and they would overcome it. However, the men who went with them would not go up against the people as they were afraid. Joshua and Caleb spoke to the congregation of the children of Israel telling them how good the land was. They said the Lord will bring us into this land and give it to us.

The congregation began to murmur against Moses and Aaron. They wanted to select a captain and return to Egypt.

The Lord appeared in the tabernacle and said to Moses, "All these men which have seen My glory, and My miracles, which I did in Egypt and in the wilderness, and have tempted Me now these ten times and have not hearkened to My voice. Surely they shall not see the land which I sware unto their fathers, neither shall any of them that provoked me see it." (Numbers 14:22-23)

The Lord said, "Caleb had a different spirit and has followed Me fully, and I will bring him into this land and his descendents will inherit it."

The Lord sent a plague and all the men, except Joshua and Caleb, ages twenty and above died in the wilderness and only their children were taken to the land God had promised to their forefathers.

Korah, Dathan, Abiram and On challenged Moses. They were joined by two hundred fifty Israelite men, well known leaders of the community. They asked

Moses and Aaron why they set themselves above the Lord's assembly. Moses said, "The Lord will show you tomorrow who belongs to Him and who is holy. Each of you come tomorrow morning to the entrance to the tent of meeting." When they were assembled, the Lord told Moses and Aaron and the community to move away from the tents of these wicked men. He then opened up the earth and it swallowed them, their families, the followers of Korah and all their property. Fire consumed the two hundred fifty men who were with Korah burning incense.

When the children of Israel came to the desert of Zin, they stayed in Kadesh. Miriam died and was buried there. They again complained to Moses and Aaron that there was no water. The Lord spoke to Moses and told him to take his rod, speak to the rock and it will give forth water. Moses was completely disgusted with the children of Israel. They gathered the congregation together before the rock, and he said, "Hear now, ye rebels; must we fetch you water out of this rock?" (Numbers 20:10) Moses hit the rock and water came out for the people and their animals. The Lord told Moses and Aaron they would not bring the congregation into the land which the Lord had given the children of Israel, as they had rebelled against the Lord's word at the water of Meribah and had not shown the Israelites how Holy He was.

Aaron died on Mount Hor and his son, Eleazar, took his place.

The Israelites moved from Mount Hor. They went around Edom and traveled toward the Red Sea. The people began to criticize Moses and the Lord, as they hated the food and were sorry they had left Egypt. This angered the Lord and He sent poisonous snakes among the people and some of them died. They asked Moses to pray to the Lord to take the snakes away. Moses prayed and the Lord answered his prayer.

King Sihon of the Amorites refused to allow the children of Israel to cross his land. They fought against the Israelites. Israel won and took possession of their land.

King Og of Bashan also fought against the Israelites. Israel won and took possession of their land.

Balak, the king of Moab, saw what the children of Israel had done to King Sihon and King Og and they were afraid. Balak sent messengers to Balaam to ask him to come and curse the Israelites. God told

Balaam to go to Balak, but to say only what He told him to say. God turned the curse into a blessing.

When they arrived at Mount Abarim, the Lord told Moses to look at the land He had promised the children of Israel. He would not be leading the children of Israel to the promised land, as he and Aaron had rebelled against the Lords word at Meribah.

The Lord told Moses to take Joshua, the son of Nun, to the priest Eleazar and give him instructions as he would lead the children to the promised land. Moses was to give the Israelites instructions regarding sacrifices, holy assemblies and vows. Moses did as the Lord commanded.

The Lord then told Moses to send troops to fight against the Midianites, as they had followed Balaam and caused the Israelites to be unfaithful to the Lord. They killed all the men, took their animals, livestock and valuables. They also burned the cities.

There was never a prophet like Moses, whom the Lord knew face to face. Moses did all the Lord commanded and gave the children of Israel all the laws, instructions and penalties the Lord expected from the children of Israel in order to obey Him, who had brought them out of Egypt.

Old Testament Saints and The Messiah

Moses spoke to all the Israelites, giving them instructions which the Lord had given him. He wrote these teachings in a book and put the book next to the Ark of the Promise for all to see. He blessed the twelve tribes of Israel. Moses was one hundred twenty years old when he died in Moab.

EIGHT

JOSHUA

Joshua was the son of Nun.

After Moses failed to believe the Lord and to satisfy Him in the eyes of the children of Israel at the waters of Meribah, the Lord told Moses he would see the land he had given the children of Israel, but he would die on the mountain and not lead the children of Israel to their land.

The Lord told Moses to take Joshua to Eleazar, the priest, to lay his hands on him and inaugurate him before all the congregation.

The Lord said, "Joshua go before the children of Israel and cause them to inherit the land I promised their fathers and I will be with you. I will never neglect or abandon you. You shall divide as an inheritance the land I swore to their fathers to give them."

Old Testament Saints and The Messiah

Joshua sent men to check out the land of Jericho. These men lodged at the house of a prostitute named Rahab. When the king heard they were there, he sent men to Rahab's house to search for them, as he knew they had come to search out the country. Rahab hid the men and sent the king's men away saying, "The men left before the gate was closed. Pursue them as they have not been gone long."

Rahab knew the Lord was with these men and had given the land to the children of Israel. She told the men she was hiding that she would help them escape if they would promise to keep her and her family safe when they took the city. The men promised Rahab when the Lord gives them the land, they will protect her and all her family. She was to put a scarlet ribbon on the window and all who stayed in her house would be safe. She let the men down by a rope from her window, and warned the men to hide in the mountains for three days until the pursuers returned.

The men returned and told Joshua the Lord had delivered all the land, as the inhabitants had lost their courage, knowing the Lord was with the children of Israel.

The next morning Joshua and all the Israelites left Shittim. They camped by the Jordan River.

The Lord held the waters of the Jordan back to let the Ark of the Covenant, the priests and the children of Israel cross on dry ground. One man from each of the twelve tribes of Israel took a stone from the middle of the Jordan, and carried them over to the place they were to lodge, to be a memorial to their children that the Jordan waters were cut off for the Ark of the Covenant of the Lord to cross. The Lord did this so the whole world would know His mighty power. When the Amorite kings and the Canaanite kings heard what the Lord had done, they had no courage to face the people of Israel. Jericho was barred shut because the people were afraid of the Israelites.

About forty thousand men, prepared for war, passed over before the Lord to the plains of Jericho.

The Lord told Joshua and his men to go around the city once each day for six days. Seven priests with trumpets will go before the Ark and on the seventh day go around the city seven times. When the trumpets make a loud blast, all the people will shout and the wall of the city will fall down. Every man shall go forward and take the city. All was destroyed except the house of Rahab, who had helped the messengers escape from the king's men when they went to spy out Jericho. Joshua told the people to take the silver, gold, vessels of brass and iron, and bring them into the treasury of the house of the Lord. He warned them not to take any accursed things as it would make the camp of Israel a curse.

The children of Israel committed a trespass regarding the accursed thing. Because of this, when Joshua sent men to Ai, they were defeated as the Lord was not with them.

The Lord told Joshua, "Israel has sinned and transgressed My covenant which I commanded them. Tell the people there is an accursed thing in their midst and you cannot stand before your enemies until you take the accursed thing from you."

Achan admitted sinning against the Lord, as he took a garment, silver and a wedge of gold. All Israel took Achan, his family and all he had to the valley of Anchor. There they stoned them to death and burned them with fire.

The men of Gibeon sent to Joshua at the camp in Gilgal asking for help. The kings of the Amorites were gathered against them. Joshua and all his fighting men went to Gilgal. The Lord appeared to

Joshua and said, "Do not fear, as I will deliver them into your hand." The Lord sent large hailstones from heaven to kill them.

The Lord told Joshua to go up against the people of Ai and He would deliver them into their hands. It came to pass, Israel took the city and brought the king of Ai back to Joshua and they hanged him.

Joshua took all the land as the Lord had commanded and gave it as an inheritance to the children of Israel, according to their divisions by tribes. When they finished dividing the land, the children of Israel gave an inheritance among them to Joshua. The Lord then gave rest unto Israel.

When Joshua was very old, he called all of Israel to him. He said, "It was the Lord who brought you to this land and you are to put away the gods your father's served, fear the Lord and serve Him in sincerity and truth."

Israel served the Lord all the days of Joshua and all the days of the elders that outlived Joshua, who had known all God did for Israel.

Joshua was one hundred ten years old when he died.

NINE

GIDEON

⚜

Gideon, who was also known as Jerubbaal, was Joash's son.

The children of Israel had done evil in the sight of the Lord and He delivered them over to the Midianites for seven years. The Midianites and Amalekites had destroyed Israel's crops and their land.

The children of Israel cried unto the Lord to deliver them. The Lord sent them a prophet to deliver His message. "I brought you out of bondage, delivered you out of the hand of the Egyptians and all your enemies, and brought you to the land I promised. However, you have not obeyed My voice."

Gideon threshed wheat by the wine press to hide it from the Midianites. The angel of the Lord appeared to him and said, "The Lord is with you." Gideon said, "If the Lord is with us, why did He forsake us and deliver us to the Midianites?"

He was called by the Lord to rescue Israel from Midian.

Gideon could not believe it was the Lord speaking to him. He asked the Lord to show him a sign to prove He was truly the Lord. The Lord gave him a sign, and Gideon knew he had seen the messenger of the Lord face to face.

The Lord told Gideon to take a bull from his father's herd and tear down the altar dedicated to Baal. He also told him to tear down the pole dedicated to the goddess Asherah. Gideon took ten of his servants by night and did as the Lord commanded.

When the people found Gideon had done this, they went to his father and told him they wanted to kill Gideon. He had destroyed the altar of Baal and cut down the grove beside it. His father said, "Are you pleading for Baal? If he is a god, let him plead for himself."

Gideon called his army together to fight against the Midianites. The Lord told him he had too many men. He told Gideon to send all the men home except three hundred men. The Lord explained to Gideon what he should do. They did as the Lord commanded, and when they blew their trumpets and broke the pitchers, the Midianites fled.

Gideon and his men chased the Midianites toward the Jordan river. They captured two Midianite princes, Oreb and Zeeb, and slew them.

They were exhausted and asked the men of Succoth for food for the men. They told them they were pursuing Zebah and Zalmunna, kings of Midian. They refused to give them food. Gideon then moved on to Penuel and asked the people there for food. They refused. After the Midianites were defeated, Gideon took the leaders of Succoth and beat them with thorns and thistles. He then tore down the tower of Penuel and killed all the men.

The men of Israel asked Gideon or his son to rule over them as he had saved them from the Midianites. Gideon told them, "Neither I, nor my son, will rule over you, as the Lord shall rule over you.".

King Zebah and King Zalmunna escaped but Gideon caught them. When he found they had killed his brothers, Gideon killed them.

Israel had peace forty years during Gideon's life. After his death at a very old age, the Israelites turned again to Baalim and made Baalberith their god. They no longer remembered the Lord their God who had delivered them out of the hands of all their enemies. They mistreated Gideon's family after all he had done for Israel.

TEN

SAMSON

✂

The people of Israel again sinned against the Lord. The Lord handed them over to the Philistines for forty years.

Manoah's wife had been unable to have a child. The Lord appeared to her and told her she was going to have a son and he would rescue Israel from the power of the Philistines. He told her never to cut his hair.

The Lord did as He promised and Manoah's wife had a son and named him Samson. The boy grew up and the Lord blessed him.

Samson met a roaring lion, but the Lord was with him and he killed the lion. Later he passed by where he had killed the lion and noticed a swarm of bees and some honey was in the dead body. He ate some of the honey and took some to his parents. He did not tell them where he got it.

Samson threw a big party when he went to marry the Philistine woman. He told all the guests a riddle and told them if they could solve it, he would give them prizes. They were unable to solve the riddle. They told Samson's wife to trick him into telling the answer to the riddle or they would kill her and her family.

Samson's wife cried and begged him to tell her the answer to the riddle. Finally, after seven days he told her the answer. She then told her friends.

After she told her friends, Samson was angry and left her. Her father gave her to their best man.

Later Samson went to see his wife. Her father refused to let him see her and told him he gave her to his best man.

Samson got three hundred foxes and tied them together by their tails. He fastened a torch between each of them, and released them in the Philistines grain fields. Their orchards also caught on fire.

The Philistines asked who did this. They were told Samson did it because his wife's father gave her to his best man. The Philistines burned Samson's wife and her father to death.

Samson attacked the Philistines, who burned his wife and her father to death, and he slaughtered them. He went to live in a cave at Etam.

Men came from Judah to the cave to capture Samson and take him to the Philistines. The Lord was still with Samson and he broke the ropes he was tied with. He took the jawbone of a donkey and killed one-thousand men.

Samson judged Israel for forty years during the Philistine rule.

He fell in love with Delilah. The Philistines asked her to trick Samson into telling her where his strength was and what made him so strong. After telling Delilah several times where his strength was, and they were not true, she continued to pester him to tell her.

He finally told her the truth and while he was sleeping, she had all his hair cut off. She called the Philistines in to attack him. They poked his eyes out and put him in a mill to grind grain.

They called for Samson to be brought to entertain them. Samson asked the Lord to give him strength one more time. When he came to the columns of the building, he asked to stop and rest awhile. He pushed on the columns on both sides of him and the building fell on the rulers and everyone in the building. Samson was also killed, but he killed more Philistines when he died than when he was alive.

ELEVEN

SAMUEL AND SAUL

~~~~

Samuel, son of Elkanah, was the last great judge of Israel and one of the first prophets.

Saul was the first king of Israel.

Elkanah had two wives, Hannah and Peninnah. Peninnah had children but Hannah had no children.

Hannah prayed to the Lord for a son, and promised the Lord she would give her son to Him all the days of his life and no razor shall come upon his head. The Lord heard and answered her prayer. She had a son and named him Samuel. She said, "The Lord has given me a son and I will lend him to the Lord as long as he lives."

Hannah and Elkanah took Samuel to the Lord's house at Shiloh while he was still a child. They left him with Eli, the priest, to serve the Lord.

The Lord again blessed Hannah and she had three sons and two daughters.

Eli had two sons, Hophni and Phinehas, who were wicked and did not serve the Lord. Eli asked his sons why they were so wicked. The priest was offered the first of the sacrifice, but Eli's sons took what they wanted first to roast for themselves. This angered the Lord as they were treating the offerings made to the Lord with contempt. The Lord spoke to Samuel one night. He told Samuel He would judge the house of Eli, as Eli's sons were evil and Eli had not restrained them. The next morning Eli asked Samuel what the Lord had said to him. Samuel told him everything the Lord had said. Eli said, "It is the Lord, let Him do what seems good to Him."

Samuel grew and the Lord was with him. All Israel knew Samuel was to be a prophet of the Lord.

Israel went out against the Philistines to battle and they were defeated. When the people came back into camp the elders wondered why the Lord had defeated them before the Philistines. The elders of Israel wanted to get the Ark of the Covenant of the Lord out of Shiloh, so it would save them from the hands of their enemies. When they went to Shiloh, the two sons of Eli, Hophni and Phinehas, were there with the Ark of the Covenant of God. When they brought it back to camp, the Philistines heard them shouting. They were afraid and said, "The Lord has come into the camp."

The Philistines again fought against Israel and defeated them. Eli's sons were killed and the Ark of God was captured. A man came to Shiloh and when he told Eli his sons were killed and the Ark of the Covenant was taken, Eli fell backwards from his seat, broke his neck and died. He was ninety eight years old and had judged Israel forty years.

The Philistines took the Ark of the Covenant of God to the house of Dagon, their god, in Ashdad, and set it by Dagon. The next morning they found Dagon had fallen. They set him up and the next morning they found Dagon had fallen again and was broken. Only a stump of Dagon was left. The hand of the Lord was heavy upon them in Ashdod and He destroyed them.

The Ark of the covenant of God was with the Philistines seven months. They sent it to Bethshemesh. The men of Bethshemesh looked into the Ark of the Lord and the Lord smote 50,310 men with a great slaughter.

The Ark of the Covenant was then sent to Eleazar, the son of Abinadab and was there for twenty years. All the house of Israel lamented after the Lord.

Samuel told the house of Israel to put away their foreign gods and serve the Lord only, then the Lord would deliver them from the hands of the Philistines. The children of Israel put away their foreign gods and served the Lord. The men of Israel pursued the Philistines and drove them back. The Philistines never returned to Israel and the Lord was against the Philistines all the days of Samuel.

Samuel had two sons, Joel and Abiah, who were judges in Beersheba. They were dishonest and perverted justice. When Samuel was old, he made his sons judges over Israel. The elders asked Samuel to give them a king to judge them, as all the other nations had kings. Samuel prayed to the Lord, and the Lord told him to do as the elders requested, as they were rejecting Him and not Samuel.

The Lord told Samuel to warn the people a king would treat them bad, and when they call out to the Lord He will not hear them.

Saul's father had lost some donkeys. He sent Saul and his servant to find them. They searched everywhere and could not find them. Saul's servant said there was a man of God in the city and possibly he could tell them which direction to go to find the donkeys.

They went into the city to find the man of God. The Lord had appeared to Samuel and told him He was sending a man from the territory of Benjamin for him to anoint king over Israel.

When Saul and his servant met Samuel, they were told to come to a banquet as his guests.

Saul spent the night on the roof at Samuel's. The next morning, Samuel anointed Saul, and told him the Lord had appointed him to be ruler over His people Israel, to save them from all their enemies.

Samuel called all the Israelites to come to him at Mizpah. He told them the Lord had chosen Saul to be their king.

Samuel wrote the laws on a scroll and placed it before the Lord. He sent the people home and Saul also went home to Gibeah.

King Nahash of Ammon poked out the right eyes of all the tribes of Gad and Reuben and would not let anyone rescue them. When Saul found out what King Nahash was doing, the spirit of the Lord came over him and he was very angry. He took a pair of oxen and cut them in pieces. He sent them throughout Israel with the message telling them this is what would happen to their oxen if they did not follow Saul and Samuel into battle. Three-hundred-thirty-thousand troops came to go to battle to save Jabash Gilead. They went into battle and defeated the Ammonites.

Samuel spoke to the people and told them they had done evil by asking for a king. However, if you give up other gods and do what is good and right, the Lord will watch over you. If you sin against God, then the people and their king will be wiped out.

Saul was thirty years old when the Lord chose him to become king and he was king for forty-two years. Saul was the son of Kish and the Lord said there was not among the children of Israel a better person than Saul.

Saul gathered three thousand men of Israel to war against the Philistines. When the men of Israel saw the great multitude of Philistines, they were afraid. Samuel was to return at a certain time to bless the troops and when he did not come, Saul was afraid, as the men had scattered from him. He then offered a burnt offering and a peace offering to the Lord. When Samuel came and saw what Saul had done, he said, "Saul, you have acted foolishly and not kept the commandment of the Lord. Therefore, the kingdom will not continue, as the Lord has chosen another to be captain over His people."

Samuel then told Saul, "Go to Amalak and destroy them and all they have." Saul and his men destroyed the Amalakites but saved the best of their animals.

The Lord came to Samuel and said, "I am sorry I chose Saul as king, as he has not performed my commandments." Samuel went to Saul and said, "Because you have rejected the word of the Lord, the Lord has rejected you from being king over Israel. He has chosen a neighbor of yours who is better than you." Saul begged Samuel to forgive his sin and return with him so he could worship the Lord. Samuel refused.

The Lord told Samuel, "I am sending Jesse, the Bethlehemite, as I have provided me a king among his sons. Take a heifer and tell Jesse you have come to sacrifice to the Lord and invite Jesse and his sons to the sacrifice."

Seven of Jesse's sons passed by Samuel and none were chosen. Samuel asked Jesse if he had other sons. Jesse said the youngest, David, is tending the sheep. Samuel said, "Send for him." The Lord told Samuel to anoint him as he was the one He had chosen. The spirit of the Lord came upon David.

TWELVE

DAVID AND SAUL

✌

Samuel sent Saul to fight against the Amalekites, and to claim everything they had for God by destroying it. He captured King Agog of Amalek and saved all the best animals and the best property.

The Lord told Samuel He regretted making Saul king. Saul had not carried out the Lord's instructions. Samuel was very angry. He got up the next morning and went to see Saul. Saul told him he had carried out the Lord's instructions. Samuel said, "You have taken the Amalekites belongings and done what the Lord considers evil." Saul begged Samuel to forgive him. Samuel told him, "The Lord has removed you from being king."

Samuel killed King Agog as he had been an evil king.

Old Testament Saints and The Messiah

The Spirit of the Lord departed from Saul, and an evil spirit from the Lord troubled him. (1 Samuel 16:14) Saul's servants called David to play the harp for Saul when the evil spirit came upon him. Saul loved David and made him his armor bearer. David returned home from Saul to feed his fathers sheep.

Jesse, the Bethlehemite, had eight sons. His three older sons followed Saul to battle. His youngest son, David, tended his father's sheep in Bethlehem.

Jesse told his son David to take food to his brothers and see if they were well.

When David arrived at their camp, Saul and his men were ready to go into battle with the Philistines. However, a giant named Goliath came out of the armies of the Philistines. He came out morning and evening for forty days and showed himself. When the men of Israel saw him they fled as they were afraid.

David went to Saul and said, "Let no man's heart fail because of him; thy servant will go and fight with this Philistine." (1 Samuel 17:32) Saul told David, "You are only a youth and the Philistine has been a man of war most of his life."

David said, "The Lord delivered me out of the paw of the lion and out of the paw of the bear. He will deliver me out of the hand of the Philistine who has defied the armies of the living God."

David chose five smooth stones from the brook and put them in his shepherd's bag. He kept his sling in his hand.

When the Philistine saw David, he cursed him by his gods. He told David to come to him and he would feed his flesh to the fowls of the air and the beasts.

David told the Philistine, "I am coming in the name of the Lord of Host's whom you have defied. Today He will deliver you into my hand and all the earth will know that there is a God in Israel."

When the Philistine came forward, David took his sling and one of the smooth stones, hit the Philistine in the forehead killing him. David had no sword, so he took the Philistines sword and cut off his head. When the Philistines saw their champion was dead, they fled.

As David and Saul returned home, the women of all the cities of Israel were singing and dancing. They said, "Saul has slain his thousands and David his ten thousands." Saul was angry when he heard this. He was also afraid of David, because the Lord was with David and had departed Saul.

Old Testament Saints and The Messiah

After the Lord rejected Saul from being king over Israel, he sent Samuel to Jesse, the Bethlehemite, as he had chosen one of his sons to be king.

Samuel went to sacrifice to the Lord and invited Jesse and his sons to the sacrifice. Samuel passed Jesse's sons in front of the Lord, but He chose none of them. Samuel asked Jesse if this was all his sons and Jesse said, " The youngest, David, is tending the sheep." Samuel said, "Send for him." When David came, the Lord told Samuel to anoint him as he was the one. Samuel anointed David and the Spirit of the Lord came upon David from that day forward.

All Israel and Judah loved David. Saul's daughter, Michal, and his son, Jonathan, loved David, but Saul became David's enemy and plotted how he could kill him.

Saul told David he would give him his daughter, Michal, if he would bring him a hundred foreskins of the Philistines. Saul thought David would fall by the hands of the Philistines. David and his men slew two-hundred Philistines and brought the foreskins back to Saul. Saul was even more afraid of David now, as he knew the Lord was with David.

Saul spoke to his son Jonathan and his servants, telling them they should kill David. Jonathan told

David that his father planned to kill him and warned him to hide.

Saul sent messengers to David's house to slay him. David's wife, Michal, told him to flee and she let him down through a window. She told the messengers David was sick. Saul sent them back to bring David on his bed. When they returned David was gone.

David fled to Nob to Ahimelech, the priest. He told the priest he was on important business for the king. David was hungry and asked the priest for bread. All the priest had was hallowed bread and he gave it to David. David then told the priest he had left on this errand in such haste he forgot his sword and asked if the priest had one he could use. The priest gave him Goliath's sword.

One of Saul's men, Doeg, saw what the priest did for David. When Saul heard this, he sent for Ahimelech and all the priests in Nob. When the priests came, Saul told his footmen to slay the priests of the Lord. The footmen would not do as Saul commanded. Saul told Doeg, the Edomite, to slay the priests. He killed many priests that day. He smote Nob, the city of the priests, and all the women, men, children and animals. Abiathar, son of Ahimelech, escaped and fled after David.

The Lord sent David and his men to Keilah to fight the Philistines. He did as the Lord said and saved Keilah.

Saul and his men went to numerous places seeking David to kill him. The Lord was with David and he always escaped before Saul and his men arrived.

Saul's men told him David was in the wilderness of Engedi. Saul took three thousand men and went to seek David. There was a cave and Saul went in to relieve himself. David and his men were in the sides of the cave. David's men encouraged David to kill Saul, as the Lord had delivered Saul into his hands. David would not kill him, but did cut off a piece of Saul's robe.

David was sad later that he had done this to the Lord's anointed. Saul left the cave and later David followed and cried out to Saul. Saul looked behind him and saw David. David bowed down and told Saul, "The Lord delivered you into my hand today. However, I have spared your life as I will not put forth my hand against you, as you are the Lord's anointed. I did cut off a piece of your robe, so you can see there is neither evil nor transgression in my hand and I have not sinned against you."

Saul then said to David, "Thou art more righteous than I; for thou has rewarded me good, whereas I have rewarded thee evil. I know thou shall surely be king and the kingdom of Israel shall be established in thine hand."(1 Samuel 24:17 and 20) He said to David, "Promise me you will not wipe out my descendents or destroy my name." So David swore to Saul.

There was a rich man in Maon, named Nabal, and his wife was Abigail. She was a very good woman, but Nabal was evil. Nabal was shearing his sheep in Carmel and David sent his men to ask Nabal for food. Nabal refused to help them. David was very angry and ready to go to war with Nabal. A servant told Abigail what Nabal had done. She gathered food and wine, and took it to David and his men before they left to attack Nabal.

When Abigail returned home, Nabal was drunk, so she did not tell him what she had done until morning. When she told Nabal what she had done, his heart died within him and he became as stone. Ten days later the Lord smote Nabal and he died.

When David heard Nabal was dead, he sent his men to Abigail, to ask her to be his wife. She became his wife. He also took Ahinoam of Jezreel to be his wife. Saul had given his daughter, Michal, to Phalti the son of Laish.

Saul continued to seek David to kill him. He was in the hill of Hachilah and David saw him sleeping, surrounded by his men. David and Abishai went in and took Saul's spear and water. None of Saul's men heard them. David went to a hill afar off and cried out to the people with Saul. He showed them the spear and water. They could have killed Saul, but again spared his life.

When Saul heard this, he said, "I have sinned: return my son David: for I will no more do thee harm because my soul was precious in thine eyes this day: behold, I have played the fool, and have erred exceedingly." (1 Samuel 26:21)

David went to Palestine territory with his six-hundred men and their families to escape Saul. King Achish of Gath let them live in Zikleg.

David and his men fought against the Geshurites, Gegrites and the Amalekites. When King Achish would ask who he raided each day, David told him they raided the portion of the Negev where the

Kenites live. This pleased the king, as he knew the people of Israel would hate David. He wanted David to be his servant. He did not know David was not telling him the truth.

The Philistines gathered their army to fight against Israel. King Achish told David to get his men ready to go with him into battle. The Philistines were angry because King Achish was allowing David and his men to go with them, so the king sent David back to Negev.

When they arrived in Negev, they discovered the Amalekites had raided the Negev, including Ziklag, and captured all the women and children.

David and four hundred men went in pursuit of the Amalekites. When they caught up with them, they attacked the Amalekites and rescued the women and children and all the loot which they had taken.

Saul went to a fortune teller and asked her to bring up Samuel, who had already died. Samuel was upset that Saul had brought him up. Saul asked Samuel to tell him what he should do, as the Philistines were making war against him and God had departed from him. Samuel said, "The Lord will deliver Israel, you and your sons into the hand of the Philistines and you will all die."

The Philistines fought against Israel and the Israelites were slain in mount Gilboa. The Philistines pursued Saul and his sons. They slew Saul's sons, Jonathan, Abinadab and Melchishua. The archers then wounded Saul. Saul asked his armor bearer to thrust the sword into him. The armor bearer refused. Saul took his sword and fell on it. When the armor bearer saw that Saul was dead, he took his sword, fell on it and died.

The men of Judah came and anointed David king over the house of Judah. David was king in Hebron over the house of Judah seven years and six months.

There was a long war between the house of Saul and the house of David, but David was stronger as the Lord was with him.

Abner asked to come to see David. David said he could come if he would bring David's wife Michal, Saul's daughter, whom Saul gave to Phaltiel after David escaped. Abner did as David requested and brought Michal back to David.

Abner communicated with the elders of Israel and said, "Ye sought for David in times past to be king over you. Now do it, for the Lord has spoken of David saying, 'By the hand of my servant David I will save my people Israel out of the hand of the

Philistines and out of the hand of all their enemies.'" (2 Samuel 3:17-18)

All the elders came to Hebron and anointed David king of Israel. David was thirty years old when he became king and reigned forty years.

After David became king, he took more concubines and wives out of Jerusalem.

The Ark of the Lord was brought into the city of David. When David danced in the streets, it angered Michal and she despised him.

As David sat in his house and the Lord had given him rest from all his enemies, he told Nathan, the prophet, he wanted to build a house for the Lord.

That night the Lord came to Nathan and told him to go to David and tell him, "When your days are fulfilled and you have gone to sleep with your fathers, I will set up your seed after you and I will establish his kingdom and he shall build my house."

David sent for Jonathan's son, Mephibosheth, who was crippled. David told him "I will restore all the land of Saul to you, and you shall eat bread at my table continually." David then called all Saul's servants and told them what he had done. He told them to till the land for him and bring in the fruits.

Zeba, Saul's servant, said they would do all the king commanded.

One day David walked out on to the roof of his house and saw a lady bathing. He sent messengers to get her. Her name was Bathsheba, the wife of Uriah. David lay with her and she conceived. She sent word to David that she was with child. David sent Uriah into battle to a place where he knew Uriah would be killed. After Uriah's wife had finished mourning for Uriah, David sent for her and she became his wife and bore him a son.

The Lord was very displeased with David. He told David He would bring evil to his house and the child born unto him will die.

After the child died, David went in to comfort Bathsheba and lay with her and she bare him another son. They called him Solomon, and the Lord loved him.

David's son Amnon, was in love with his sister, Tamar. He pretended to be sick and requested that Tamar be allowed to come and cook for him. When she brought his food, he took hold of her and forced her to lay with him.

When his brother Absolom heard this, he was determined to kill Amnon.

After two years, Absolom had sheepshearers in Baalhazor and he invited all the king's sons to go with him to Baalhazor. He commanded his servants to kill Amnon as soon as he was merry with wine. His servants did as he commanded. Absolom fled to Geshur and stayed there three years.

Finally David sent Joab to get Absolom to return to Jerusalem, but David said he did not want to see Absolom. However, after two years, David finally agreed to see Absolom. Absolom bowed to the king and the king kissed him.

Absolom began to plot against David. All Israel, who came to the king for judgment, were met by Absolom who always gave them justice. He stole the hearts of the men of Israel. After forty years he asked David to let him go to Hebron to serve the Lord. David said, "Go in peace."

A messenger came to David and said, "The hearts of the men of Israel are after Absolom." (2 Samuel 15:13) David and his men fled to escape Absolom.

David went to the top of the Mount of Olives and was met by Ziba, Mephibosheth's servant. He brought them saddled donkeys to ride, and bread, raisens, fruit and wine. Absolom thought David and his men would be exhausted and hungry and easy to defeat. David called his troops together and put three commanders in charge. Each commander took one-third of the troops with them. They fought against Absolom and his men, and defeated them.

David's men would not let David go to war with them. David told his men not to hurt Absolom. However, Absolom was on a mule and it went under a tree limb. Absolom was caught on the tree limb, but the mule went on. Joab saw this and put three darts into Absolom's heart and he died. The Lord was still with David and his men defeated Absolom's army. David wept and mourned for Absolom when he heard he was dead.

Every man from Israel followed Sheba, the son of Bichri, but the men of Judah from Jordan to Jerusalem followed David. David sent Amasa to assemble the men of Judah to pursue Sheba. Amasa did not do as David instructed and when Joab and Abishai overtook Amasa, Joab killed him.

Joab and Abishai pursued after Sheba. They besieged him in Abel and all the people with Joab battered the wall to tear it down. A lady spoke to Joab and said, "I am peaceable and faithful in Israel." She asked Joab not to destroy their city. Joab told her if she would send Sheba out, they would not harm the city. They cut off Sheba's head and threw it over the wall. Joab and his men returned to Jerusalem.

The Lord delivered David out of the hand of all his enemies and David sang a song of thanksgiving to the Lord.

King David was old and very ill. His son Adonijah, the son of Haggith, exalted himself, saying, "I will be king." (1Kings 1:5) He began to reign and King David did not know this. Bathsheba went in to the king and said, "My lord, thou swarest by the Lord thy God unto thine handmaid, saying, 'Assuredly Solomon thy son shall reign after me, and he shall sit upon my throne.' Now, behold, Adonijah reigneth and now, my Lord the king, thou knowest not." (1 Kings 1:17-18)

The king called the priest, and the prophet and told them to take the servants and go to Gihon and let Zadok, the priest, and Nathan, the prophet, anoint Solomon the king over Israel. David instructed Solomon to always walk in the ways of the Lord, to keep His statutes, commandments, judgments and testimonials as written in the Law of Moses. King David got to see his son sit on the throne and he praised the Lord God of Israel.

King David ruled as king of Israel for forty years. He ruled seven years in Hebron and thirty-three years in Jerusalem. David slept with his fathers and was buried in the City of David.

THIRTEEN

SOLOMON

Solomon was the son of David and Bathsheba.

King David had his son, Solomon, anointed king over Israel before his death. He instructed Solomon to be strong and mature, and to obey all of God's laws.

Solomon married Pharaoh's daughter and brought her into the city of David where he built his house, the Lord's house and the wall around Jerusalem.

The Lord appeared to Solomon in a dream at Gibeon. The Lord asked Solomon what He could give him. Solomon said, "Give thy servant an understanding heart to judge thy people, that I may discern between good and bad; for who is able to judge this thy so great a people?" (1 Kings 3:9)

Old Testament Saints and The Messiah

The Lord was pleased with this request and told Solomon, "I will give you a wise and understanding heart, riches and honor." People came from every nation to hear King Solomon's wisdom. They came from all the kings of the earth who had heard about his wisdom.

Solomon had dominion over all the region, from Tiphsah to Gaza, and over all the kings. He had peace on every side, all around him. Judah and Israel dwelt safely all the days of Solomon.

Solomon wanted to build a house for the Lord. The Lord told his father, David, not to build a house for Him. He said David would have a son and he would build the house for the Lord.

Hiram, king of Tyre, agreed to furnish timber of cedar and fir. The timber was floated down the sea on floats to the building site. Solomon furnished thousands of men to work on this project. He gave Hiram food for his household year after year.

Solomon had been king for four years when he began building the house of the Lord. The word of the Lord came to Solomon, saying, "Concerning this house which thou art in building, if thou wilt walk in My statutes, and execute My judgments, and keep all My commandments to walk in them; then will

I perform my word with thee, which I spake unto David, thy father. And I will dwell among the children of Israel, and will not forsake My people Israel." (1 Kings 6:11-13)

It took Solomon seven years to build the house of the Lord. It took him thirteen years to finish his own house. Solomon brought all the things his father dedicated, the silver, gold and vessels and put them among the treasures of the house of the Lord.

The priest brought the Ark of the Lord to the house, to the most holy place. A cloud filled the house of the Lord, for the glory of the Lord had filled the house.

When the temple was finished, Solomon prayed a prayer of dedication to the Lord, with his hands spread up toward heaven. He then stood and blessed all the congregation of Israel.

The queen of Sheeba heard of Solomon's wisdom and wealth. She could not believe all the good things she heard. She came to Jerusalem with gold, precious stones and spices for Solomon so she could talk with him. After talking with Solomon, she was convinced of his wisdom, the happiness of all his servants and his prosperity.

Solomon exceeded all the kings of the earth for riches and wisdom. Everyone sought Solomon to hear his wisdom, which God had put in his heart.

But King Solomon loved many strange women, together with the daughter of Pharaoh, women of the Moabites, Amonites, Edomites, Zidonians and Hittites. (1 Kings 11:1) The Lord told Solomon and all the children of Israel not to go in to these women, as he said, "They will turn away your hearts to their gods."

Solomon had seven hundred wives who were princesses and three hundred concubines. His wives turned his heart away to their gods. Solomon went after Ashtoreth, the goddess of the Sidonians, and after Milcom, the abomination of the Ammonites. He did evil in the sight of the Lord, and did not follow the Lord as his father did.

Solomon did evil in the sight of the Lord. The Lord was angry with Solomon since he had not kept the Lord's covenant and His statutes. The Lord told him, "I will take the kingdom from you and give it to your servant. However, I will not do this for David's sake, so I will give one tribe to your son." The Lord gave ten tribes to Jeroboam. Solomon sought to kill

Jerobaum. Jerobaum fled to Egypt until the death of Solomon.

Solomon reigned in Jerusalem over all Israel for forty years. He slept with his fathers and was buried in the City of David. Rehoboam, his son, reigned in his place.

FOURTEEN

ELIJAH

⚜

Elijah, the Tishbite, was a prophet from Gilead who obeyed the Lord in all things.

Ahab, the king of Israel, did evil in the sight of the Lord. He was the worst of all kings. He took Jezebel as his wife and began worshipping and serving Baal.

The Lord told Elijah to tell Ahab there would be no rain for the next few years until the Lord tells him to let it rain. The Lord told Elijah to hide beside the brook Cherith and he could drink from the brook. The Lord commanded the ravens to feed Elijah.

The brook dried up, since there was no rain, and the Lord told Elijah to go to Zarephath and dwell there.

Old Testament Saints and The Messiah

The Lord had commanded a widow to sustain Elijah. Elijah asked the widow for some bread and water. She said she only had a handful of meal and a little oil. She was gathering wood to prepare something for herself and her son so they could eat then die. Elijah told her, "Go and make a cake for me and after that make some for yourself and your son." The Lord said, "Until the Lord sends rain on the land, the jar of flour will never be empty and the jug will always contain oil." Elijah, the widow and her son ate for many days.

The widow's son became very ill and there was no breath left in him. Elijah took the boy upstairs and prayed to the Lord to heal him. The Lord heard Elijah's prayer and healed the boy.

Jezebel slew the prophets of the Lord. Obadiah was a devout Christian and he took one hundred prophets, hid them in caves, and kept them alive by feeding them with bread and water.

After three years, the Lord told Elijah, "Go to Ahab and I will send rain upon the earth."

Ahab came to meet Elijah. Elijah told him to gather all the children of Israel, the prophets of the groves which eat at Jezebel's table, and send them to Mount Carmel. Give us two bulls, one bull for yourself and one bull for me. Cut your bull in pieces and lay it on the wood but do not set it on fire. I will do the same with my bull.

Elijah said to the children of Israel, "Call upon your gods to send fire, then I will call upon my God to bring fire and the god that answers by fire, let him be God." The prophets of Baal cried out to their god from morning to noon and to the evening sacrifice. They received no answer.

Elijah said to all the people, "Come over here." Elijah built an altar in the Lord's name and placed twelve stones (one for each of Jacob's sons) on it. He placed the bull on the wood and poured water on his bull and on the wood. He then called out to his God to let it be known that He was the God of Israel. The fire of the Lord fell and consumed the burnt sacrifice, the wood, the stones, the dust and licked up the waters in the trench.

When the people saw this they fell on their faces and declared, "The Lord is God."

Elijah told the people to take the prophets of Baal to the brook Kishon and slaughter them.

When Ahab told Jezebel what Elijah had done, she sent a messenger to tell Elijah she was going to have him killed. Elijah fled to Beersheba, left his servant there, and he went into the wilderness.

He asked the Lord to take his life, as he was no better than his ancestors. He lay down under a juniper tree and slept. Behold, an angel appeared as he slept and said, "Arise and eat." There was a cake and water so he ate and drank then went back to sleep. Again, an angel appeared to him and said, "Arise and eat as you are going on a long journey." He ate and drank and went forty days and nights in that strength to Horeb the mount of God. He came to a cave and lodged there.

The Lord appeared to Elijah and told him to go to the wilderness of Damascus and anoint Hazael to be king over Syria, anoint Jehu to be king over Israel, and anoint Elisha to be a prophet. The Lord said, "I have left seven thousand in Israel who have not bowed to Baal."

Ahab went to Naboth and asked him to give him his vineyard as it was beside Ahab's home. He told Naboth he would give him another vineyard or money. Naboth refused and Ahab was very sad. Jezebel sent letters and signed Ahab's name, to all the elders and nobles, saying Naboth had blasphemed God and the king. They carried Naboth out and stoned him to death. Jezebel told Ahab to take possession of the vineyard as Naboth was dead.

The word of the Lord came to Elijah, saying, "Go meet Ahab and ask if he killed Naboth and took possession of his vineyard. Tell him I will bring evil to his house and the dogs shall eat Jezebel by the wall of Jezreel."

When Ahab heard this, he humbled himself before the Lord. The Lord said, since he humbled himself, he would not bring evil in Ahab's days, but would bring evil upon his son's house.

However, during the war with Syria, Ahab was hit and his blood ran onto the chariot and the dogs licked his blood. The king died and his body was brought to Samaria and buried.

Moab rebelled against Israel after the death of Ahab. Ahaziah, the son of Ahab, began to reign over Israel in Samaria.

Ahaziah fell and was very sick. He sent messengers to ask Baalzebub if he would recover. The Lord sent Elijah to the messenger to tell him Ahaziah would die.

The king sent fifty men to tell Elijah to come down. The Lord sent fire down from heaven to consume the fifty men. The king then sent fifty more men to tell Elijah to come down quickly. The Lord sent fire down from heaven and consumed this fifty men.

When Ahaziah sent another fifty men, they begged Elijah to come to the king and not harm them. Elijah went to the king and told him he would die. He died according to the word of the Lord which Elijah had spoken.

Elisha went with Elijah to Bethel, Jericho and to the Jordan. Elijah took his mantle and wrapped it together and smote the waters. The waters were divided and Elijah and Elisha went across on dry ground.

Elijah asked Elisha what he could do for him before he was taken away. Elisha said, "I pray thee, let a double portion of thy spirit be upon me." (2 Kings 2:9) As Elijah and Elisha went on, there appeared a chariot of fire, and Elijah went up by a whirlwind into heaven. (This is an Old Testament rapture of a saint of God, just as it will happen to the New Testament believers when the Lord Jesus Christ returns at the rapture.) Elisha saw this and he took Elijah's mantle that had fallen from him. Elisha went to the bank of the Jordan, smote the water and it parted. Elisha crossed on dry ground.

FIFTEEN

ELISHA

⁂

Elijah anointed Elisha as a prophet and he followed Elijah until he was taken up into heaven by a whirlwind.

Elijah asked Elisha what he could do for him before he was taken up into heaven. Elisha said, "I pray thee, let a double portion of thy spirit be upon me." (2 Kings 2:9)

As Elisha was in Jericho, the men of the city came to him as the water was bad and the ground was barren. Elisha told the men to bring him a jar with salt in it. He threw the salt in the water and the water was healed. The Lord healed the waters and said there would be no more barren land.

Mesha, the king of Moab, rebelled against the king of Israel. King Jehoram, king of Israel, sent for

Jehoshaphat, king of Judah and the king of Edom and all of them went out against Moab. They traveled seven days and there was no water for them or their cattle. Jehoshaphat asked if there was a prophet they could inquire of the Lord by him. A servant of the king of Israel mentioned Elisha. They went to Elisha and the Lord spoke to Elisha and said, "Make this valley full of ditches. There will be no wind or rain but the valley shall be filled with water. Tell the kings I will deliver the Moabites into their hands."

A wife of one of the sons of the prophets came to Elisha. She said a creditor had come to take her two sons as bondmen. Elisha asked her what she had in her house. She said, "Only a pot of oil." Elisha told her to gather all the empty vessels from her neighbors. When they were full of oil, Elisha told her to go sell the oil and pay her debt.

Elisha met a woman in Shunam, who invited him in to eat bread when he passed by. She told her husband, "I know this is a man of God, so let's make a chamber with bed, table, stool and a candlestick for him." When Elisha saw what they had done for him, he called the woman and asked what he could do for her. She asked for nothing. Elisha's servant, Gehazi, said, "She has no child and her husband is

Old Testament Saints and The Messiah

old." Elisha called to the woman again and told her according to the time of life she would embrace her son. She conceived and bore a son.

When the boy was grown, he was in the field with his father when he got a severe headache. They took him to his mother, but he died. She laid him on Elisha's bed, closed the door and went after Elisha. She told him what had happened. Elisha gave his servant his staff and told him to rush to the Shunammite's house and lay it on the face of the boy. When Elisha arrived, he went up to the boy and prayed to the Lord. He lay on the boy to warm him and he came alive. When Elisha took him to his mother, she fell at his feet and bowed herself to the ground.

Naaman, captain of the host of the king of Syria, was a great man. By him the Lord had given deliverance to Syria, but he was a leper. His wife's handmaid told her there was a prophet in Samaria who could heal Naaman. Naaman took a letter to the king of Israel, asking to be healed of leprosy. The king had no power to do this, but when Elisha heard, he sent word to the king to send the leper to him, then he would know there is a prophet in Israel.

Naaman came with his horses and his chariot and stood at the door of the house of Elisha. Elisha sent a messenger to the door to tell Naaman to go to the Jordan river and dip himself seven times and he would be healed. Naaman was upset because Elisha did not come to the door, or call upon the name of the Lord his God to heal him. His servants came to him and persuaded him to do as the prophet said. He went to the Jordan river and dipped himself seven times and was healed. He went to Elisha and said he knew there was no other God in all the earth but in Israel. Naaman offered a blessing to Elisha, but Elisha refused to take it.

After Naaman left, Gehazi, Elisha's servant, ran after Naaman. He told Naaman Elisha had sent him. He said there were two sons of the prophets from Mount Ephraim and he asked for a talent of silver and two changes of clothes for these men. Naaman gave him two talents of silver and two changes of garments. When Elisha saw what Gehazi had done, he told Gehazi that Naaman's leprosy would cleave to him and his seed forever.

The sons of the prophets asked Elisha to go with them to Jordan. They cut wood and were making it a land where they could dwell. While they were cutting wood, an ax fell into the water. Elisha cast a stick in the water, the ax floated and they retrieved it.

Old Testament Saints and The Messiah

The king of Aram was fighting against Israel. The man of God sent a message to the king of Israel telling him where the Arameans were staying so he would not go there. The king of Aram thought there was a spy among his men. The officer told him, "Elisha, the prophet, tells the king of Israel everything you say, even what you say in your bedroom."

The king was very angry when he heard this and demanded his men find Elisha so he could capture him. When he was told Elisha was in Dotham, he sent horses, chariots and a large fighting unit there. As they came down to capture Elisha, the Lord struck them with blindness. Elisha led them to Samaria and asked the Lord to restore their sight. When the king of Israel saw them, he asked Elisha if he should kill them. Elisha said, "Feed them and send them back to their master." After this, the Aramean troops never raided Israel's territory again.

Elisha carried on Elijah's work as the Lord's prophet in Israel for fifty years. God allowed Elisha to perform many miracles.

SIXTEEN

HEZEKIAH

⚜

There were many evil kings in Judah and Jerusalem after Elisha's death.

The Lord warned Judah and Israel to turn from their evil ways and obey His commands. They refused to listen and abandoned all the commands of the Lord their God. The Lord became so angry that He removed them from His sight. Only the tribe of Judah was left.

The people of Israel made Jeroboam king. The Israelites followed all the sins of Jeroboam, so the Lord turned away from Israel and the people were taken as captives by the Assyrians.

When Hezekiah, son of Ahaz, became king of Israel, he was twenty-five years old. He did what the Lord considered right. Hezekiah's mother was Abijah, the daughter of Zechariah.

He got rid of the illegal places of worship, cut down the poles dedicated to the goddess Asherah, and had the temple of the Lord repaired and cleansed.

He rebelled against the king of Assyria and would not serve him. He conquered the Philistines and the fortified cities all the way to Gaza and it's territory.

Hezekiah opened the doors of the Lord's temple and repaired them. He assembled the priests and Levites in the square and told them to consecrate themselves and the temple of the Lord. They removed all that had been corrupted from the Holy Place. After they had completed the cleansing, they brought sacrifices and thank offerings.

Hezekiah told the people, "Your father's did evil in the eyes of the Lord. Therefore, the Lord made Judah and Jerusalem a place of horror and scorn. Our fathers were killed in battle and our sons, daughters and wives are prisoners because of this. I will make a covenant to the Lord God of Israel, so He will turn His burning anger from us."

Messengers took letters from the king throughout Israel and Judah, inviting the people to come to Jerusalem to celebrate the Passover of the Lord God

Old Testament Saints and The Messiah

of Israel. Many people came and the city of Jerusalem was full of joy. Nothing like this had happened in Jerusalem since the days of King Solomon of Israel.

Hezekiah obeyed all the commands the Lord had given through Moses. The Lord was with him and he succeeded in everything he did.

Sennacherib, the king of Assyria, sent men to Jerusalem to tell the people to surrender to them, as they were not strong enough to defeat Assyria and their god was like all the others they had defeated. He could not help them.

When Hezekiah saw Sennacherib had come to wage war against Jerusalem, he, his officers and his military staff stopped the waters flowing out of the streams. They did not want the king of Assyria to have water. They repaired the walls, made weapons and shields. Hezekiah told his military commanders, "Be strong and courageous as the Lord is on our side and will help us fight our battles."

When Hezekiah heard this, he went into the Lord's temple along with the prophet Isaiah, and they prayed and cried out to the Lord. The Lord sent an angel to cut off the Assyrians. When King Sennacherib returned to Assyria, his people slew him with a sword.

The Lord heard his plea and saved Hezekiah and Jerusalem from the hand of the king of Assyria and all their enemies.

Hezekiah became very ill. Isaiah, the prophet, came to him. He told him he was going to die. Hezekiah wept and asked the Lord to heal him. The Lord had mercy on him and told him He would give him another fifteen years.

The king of Babylon sent letters and a present to Hezekiah when he heard he was sick. Hezekiah was so pleased, he showed the Babylonians his silver, gold, everything in his treasury, and everything in his palace.

When Isaiah heard what Hezekiah had done, he said, "The day will come when the Babylonians will take everything in your palace and put it in the palace of the king of Babylon.

Hezekiah lived in peace and security all of his life.

When Hezekiah died, his son, Manasseh, succeeded him as king.

Manasseh was an evil king and did not follow the Lord's commands.

He rebuilt the illegal places of worship his father had torn down. He set up altars dedicated to other

Old Testament Saints and The Messiah

---

gods and made a pole dedicated to the goddess Asherah. He burned his son as a sacrifice, practiced witchcraft and consulted fortune tellers.

When the Lord spoke to Manasseh and his people, they would not listen. The Lord made the army commanders of the king of Assyria invade Judah. They took Manasseh captive, put him in shackles and took him to Babylon.

Manasseh begged the Lord to bring him back to Jerusalem. The Lord heard his plea and brought him back to his kingdom in Jerusalem.

After this, Manasseh knew that the Lord is God. He got rid of the foreign gods and the illegal places of worship.

When Manasseh died, they buried him in his own palace.

SEVENTEEN

EZRA

❧

Ezra was the son of Seraiah.

The Lord stirred up the spirit of King Cyrus, king of Persia, and he told all the people he wanted them to go to Jerusalem and build the house of the Lord.

The chief of the fathers of Judah and Benjamin, the priests and the Levites went to Jerusalem to build the house of the Lord. Those who chose not to go were to give silver, gold, beasts and farewell offerings for the house of God in Jerusalem.

Cyrus, the king, brought the vessels, which Nebuchadnezzar had taken when he took the children of Israel into bondage, and gave them to be put in the house of the Lord. He gave them silver and gold from himself and his counselors, also vessels, wheat, wine and oil to use in the house of the Lord.

Old Testament Saints and The Messiah

He made it unlawful for a toll, tribute or custom to be imposed upon them.

Ezra knew that God was with him as he led the group of Jews back to Jerusalem. They prayed and fasted before they left, as they knew it would be a long, dangerous journey. When they arrived in Jerusalem, they offered sacrifices to God.

There was much silver and gold and Sheshbazzar, the prince of Judah, brought these to Jerusalem to be put in the house of the Lord.

The people built the altar first, then the foundation. When the foundation was laid, they played music and sang praises to the Lord for His goodness and mercy.

When the adversaries of Judah and Benjamin heard the children of Israel were building the house of the Lord, they hired counselors against them to frustrate their purpose. This occurred all through the reign of Cyrus, king of Persia.

When Artaxerxes, king of Persia began to reign, they wrote letters complaining that the Jews were building the temple and the walls. They said when complete, they will not pay toll, tribute and custom. The king told them to go to the Jews in Jerusalem and tell them to cease work on the walls and the temple.

Old Testament Saints and The Messiah

The work ceased until the second year of the reign of Darius, king of Persia.

Their adversaries asked who gave them permission to build the house and the walls. The elders answered them, saying, "We are the servants of heaven and earth. Our fathers provoked the God of heaven and He gave them to Nebuchadnezzar, the king of Babylon, and the Chaldeans, who destroyed this house. King Cyrus made a decree for us to build this house of God."

The workers refused to stop working. They sent a letter to the king asking him to search the treasures of the house of King Darius, and they would find a decree he made for them to build the house of God in Jerusalem.

Darius, king of Persia, found the decree King Cyrus had written. He wrote a decree himself, stating no one was to stop work again on the house of God. If anyone tried to stop this work, they would be punished severely. He also commanded them to give money for the workers expenses, animals for burnt offerings and anything else they need daily.

When the house of the Lord was complete, the children of Israel, the priests, the Levites and the rest of the children of captivity kept a dedication to the house of God with joy.

Ezra was well versed in the laws of God and taught the people of Israel the statutes and judgments.

The people gathered at the water gate and Ezra read the book of the Law of Moses, which the Lord had commanded Israel. They confessed their sins and the sins of their fathers and gave thanks to the Lord for all He had done for them. They made an oath to walk in God's laws, which were given by Moses, and to observe and do all the commandments of the Lord and His judgments and statutes.

The princes came to Ezra and told him the people, priests and Levites had not separated themselves from the people of the land and were doing according to their abominations. They have taken their daughters for themselves and their sons.

God had told the people not to give their sons or daughters or accept sons or daughters from these people, as they have filled their land with abomination from one end to the other with their uncleanness.

Ezra was very distraught when he heard this and he began to pray. He said, "God delivered the people from bondage and extended mercy so they could rebuild the house of God and the walls in Jerusalem.

This is what tore the nation apart when the people were separated into two nations and held captives." The congregation of men, women and children wept.

Shechaniah, the son of Jehiel, spoke to Ezra saying they had transgressed against God. He suggested they make a covenant with God that all who had taken wives, should give them and their children back. God moved the heart of the people and they agreed to put away their strange wives and children they had acquired against God's will.

Ezra called all the people from Judah and Jerusalem to gather in Jerusalem within three days. All the men of Judah and Benjamin came within three days. Ezra stood up and said, "You have transgressed against the Lord, now make confession to the Lord and separate yourselves from the people of this land and from the strange wives." All who had taken strange wives sent them back to their land, along with the children born to them.

EIGHTEEN

NEHEMIAH

✤

Nehemiah was the son of Hachaliah. He was a man of great faith and leadership.

He was a cup bearer for King Artaxerxes of Persia.

When he heard the children of Israel were in great affliction, the walls of Jerusalem were broken down and the gates had been burned, he wept. He prayed and asked God to have compassion on his people.

He began to pray for the Lord to touch the king's heart, so the king would allow him to go to Jerusalem to rebuild the walls.

When he went before the king to give him his wine, the king noticed Nehemiah was sad. He asked him why he was sad. He told the king what had happened to the walls and gates in Jerusalem and how the people were afflicted. When he told the king what he wanted to do, the king granted him leave to go to Jerusalem to rebuild the walls. The king also furnished him with timber. King Artaxerxes was not a follower of the God of Israel, however, he was married to a Jew and had sympathy for them.

Nehemiah was appointed governor of Jerusalem. After Nehemiah and the people began rebuilding the walls, Sanballot and Tobiah tried to stop the building of the walls. They did not want Jerusalem to be strong and fortified again.

They began to plot an attack on Jerusalem. Nehemiah prayed and stationed guards along the wall twenty-four hours each day. The workers were placed on the part of the wall closest to their homes. Nehemiah told the workers not to fear, as God would fight for them, and if they heard the sound of the trumpet it would mean trouble and they should come immediately.

Nehemiah's enemies tried to trick him into meeting with them in the village of the Ono valley. They planned to harm him. Nehemiah refused to go and told them his job was too important to leave.

His enemies then sent a false prophet to ask Nehemiah to go into the temple to avoid being killed.

Nehemiah was not a priest and could not legitimately enter the temple. He realized God did not send this man so he refused to go to the temple.

The walls and gates were finished in fifty-two days. When their enemies heard this, they were afraid, as they knew this work was done with the help of God.

Thousands of exiles returned to Jerusalem and Judah. All the people gathered at the water gate and Ezra read the Law of Moses to them. The people confessed, worshipped God and thanked Him for all His blessings. They made a covenant with God, to walk in God's law which was given by Moses, and to do all the commandments of the Lord.

They promised not to give their daughters to the people of the land, nor take their daughters for their sons. They promised not to buy or sell on the Sabbath or Holy days. Other ordinances were made. The people charged themselves to provide whatever was needed in the house of God and not to forsake it.

The rulers of the people dwelt in Jerusalem, and the rest of the people cast lots. One of each ten people would dwell in Jerusalem and the others would dwell in other cities. Everyone was told their duties and station.

When they read the book of Moses it said, "No Ammonite or Moabite should be allowed in the congregation of God forever. They did not help the children of Israel when they were in the wilderness. They hired Balaam to curse the Israelites, however, the Lord turned it into a blessing."

Eliashib, the priest, allowed Tobiah to live in a large room in the house of God.

Nehemiah had gone back to Persia to see the king. He again asked the king for permission to go back to Jerusalem to see if all was going as committed. He was granted permission.

When Nehemiah found Eliasheb had allowed Tobiah to move into a chamber in the courts of the house of God, he was furious. He threw all of Tobiah's household goods outside. He commanded them to cleanse the chambers so everything could be moved back into the house of God.

Nehemiah also found the Levites and singers had fled to their homes because they were not being paid. Nehemiah asked the rulers why the house of the Lord had been forsaken. He gathered them all together and set them in their place.

In Judah the people were treading wine presses on the Sabbath. They were selling animals and fruit on the Sabbath in Jerusalem.

Nehemiah reminded the people their fathers did these things and God brought evil upon them and the city. He demanded the gates be locked in the evening before the Sabbath and not opened until the day after the Sabbath.

Jew's were taking wives of the Ashdods, Ammonites and Moabites. This was one of God's commandments in the book of Moses, that the people should not give their daughters to these people or take their daughters for their sons. Nehemiah cleansed them of all these strangers and prayed for God's forgiveness.

NINETEEN

ESTHER

✢

Ahasuerus was king and he gave a party for his princes, servants and nobles. Vashti, the queen, made a feast for the women in the royal house.

On the seventh day of the party, the king was merry with wine, and he commanded the seven chamberlains to bring his wife, Vashti, so he could show the people and princes how beautiful she was. The queen refused to come at the king's request. He became very angry. One of his chamberlains said, "If you do not do something about her rebuff, then all the women will feel they can do this to their husbands." The king agreed and told them to send her away and he would give her royal estate to someone better than she.

The king told the chamberlains to find beautiful virgins and bring them so he could choose another queen.

Esther had no father or mother, so Mordecai took her and raised her as his own daughter. She was the daughter of Mordecai's uncle. Esther was very beautiful and when Mordecai heard the king was looking for a queen, he took Esther to the king's house.

The king loved Esther more than the other virgins, so he placed the royal crown on her head and made her queen.

Mordecai sat by the king's gate each day to see what would happen to Esther. While he was waiting one day, he overheard two of the king's chamberlains plotting to do harm to the king. He told Esther and she told the king. The two men were tried, found guilty and were hanged.

The king chose to promote Haman to be above all the princes. The king's servants, who were in the king's gate, bowed and reverenced Haman, but Mordecai did not. This angered Haman and he knew Mordecai was a Jew, so he wanted to destroy all the Jews who were throughout the kingdom. Haman went to the king and told him there were people within the kingdom whose laws were diverse from all the people and they do not keep the king's laws. He asked the king to let it be that they be destroyed. The king took his ring from his finger and gave it to Haman. He told Haman to do with these people whatever he wanted.

A letter was written to all the lieutenants, governors and rulers of all the provinces that they should kill all the Jews, even women and children.

When Esther heard this she was grieved. Mordecai tore his clothes and put on sackcloth with ashes. Esther sent clothes to Mordecai but he never received them.

Esther sent for one of the king's chamberlains and told him to go to Mordecai and see what was happening. Mordecai told him Haman had promised a sum of money to the king's treasuries if he could destroy the Jews. He gave him a copy of the decree to show Esther. Tell her to go to the king and request him to save her people.

She said she was not allowed to go before the king unless she was called and she might be put to death if she went to him. Mordecai said she would also be killed if all the Jews were killed.

After fasting for three days, Esther put on her royal apparel and stood in the inner court of the king's house. When the king saw her, he held out the scepter to show her she could enter his presence. He asked what her request was and said it would be given to her, even to half of the kingdom. She invited the king and Haman to a banquet she was preparing the next day.

The king couldn't sleep that night and he asked them to bring the book of records of the chronicles and read it to him. It was written that Mordecai had told about the two men who planned an attack on the king. The king asked what honor or dignity was done for Mordecai for this. They told the king nothing had been done for him.

Haman had built a gallows on which to hang Mordecai. He came to the king to ask if he could hang Mordecai. Before he could ask the king, the king asked him what he could do for a man he wanted to honor. Haman thought the king was talking about him. He told the king what he should do. The king agreed and told Haman to get apparel and put it on Mordecai, get him a horse to ride through the city and tell everyone this is what will be done for the man whom the king delights to honor.

Haman was devastated. He went home and told his wife what happened. While they were talking, the king's chamberlain came to get Haman to take him to the banquet Queen Esther had prepared for them.

The king asked Esther what her request was. She asked that her life be saved and that of her people. My people have been sold to be destroyed and slain. The king asked her who did this. She said, "It was the wicked Haman."

The king was furious. He told his chamberlains to hang Haman from the gallows he had built for Mordecai.

After Haman was executed, the king gave Haman's estate to Esther.

Esther told the king what Mordecai was to her. He gave Mordecai his ring and set him over the house of Haman.

Esther again asked the king to save her people. He told Esther and Mordecai to write a letter and send it throughout the provinces that the Jew's were not to be harmed. The Jew's were told to gather with each other and fight against anyone who tried to harm them.

Haman's ten sons were hanged at Esther's request. Mordecai was advanced to a position next to the king and was great among the Jews.

TWENTY

JOB

⚜

Job lived in Uz. He was perfect and upright, one who feared and obeyed God and turned away from evil.

He had seven sons and three daughters. He had great wealth, prestige and many servants. He had many sheep, camels, oxen and a very great household. Job was considered the greatest man in the East, because of the wealth he had accumulated.

Job's sons and daughters would gather together to eat and drink. Job offered burnt offerings each time for their sins.

The sons of God came to present themselves before the Lord and satan also came. God told satan there was none like Job in all the earth as he was upright, feared the Lord and shunned evil. Satan said,

"You have made a hedge around him and blessed him on every side, but if you put forth your hand and take this away he will curse you to your face." The Lord told satan to do what he wanted to Job, but to spare his life. The Lord knew Job would not lose his faith, no matter what satan did.

A messenger came to Job telling him the Sabeans took his animals and killed his servants. Another messenger came to Job to tell him fire of God fell from the heavens and burned all his sheep and his servants. Still another messenger came to Job to tell him the Chaldeans had taken all the camels and slain his servants. A fourth messenger came to tell Job his sons house was destroyed and all his children were dead.

In all of this Job sinned not, nor blamed the Lord for these things. He fell down on the ground and worshipped God. He said, "The Lord giveth and the Lord can take away."

The sons of God came again to present themselves before the Lord and satan came also to the Lord and said, "If you put forth your hand and touch Job's bone and his flesh, he will curse you to your face." The Lord told satan to do what he wanted to Job, but to spare Job's life.

Old Testament Saints and The Messiah

Satan smote Job with boils from his head to his feet. Job shaved his head and put on sackcloth and ashes.

Job's wife told him to curse God and die. Job said, "Shall we receive good at the hand of God and not receive evil?"

Three of Job's friends came to comfort him when they heard what had happened to him. When they saw Job, they barely recognized him, as his head was shaved, his clothes torn and he had sores all over his body. When they saw how great his grief was, they sat with him seven days and nights without speaking.

Job finally spoke and cursed the day he was born. He wished he had died at birth and would gladly die now to escape the suffering he was having to endure.

Job's friend, Eliphaz, the Temanite, spoke to Job. He said, no one perishes being innocent. "By the blast of God they perish, and by the breath of His nostrils they are consumed." (Job 4:9) "Behold, happy is the man whom God correcteth; therefore, despise not the chastening of the Almighty." (Job 5:17)

Job answered and said, "The arrows of the almighty are within me, the poison whereof drinketh up my spirit and the terrors of God set themselves in array against me." (Job 6:4)

Job asked the Lord why these afflictions had come upon him. God did not answer. God wanted satan to see that Job was a righteous and believing servant and that none of these things would turn him away from God.

Another of Job's friends spoke. Bildad said Job and his family suffered because of their sins. He told Job he should seek God and make supplication to the Almighty.

Then the other friend spoke to Job. He was Zophar, the Naamathite. He told Job if iniquity was in his hand, he should put it far away and lift up his face without spot.

Job told his friends they were unable to render a diagnosis and incapable of prescribing the proper cure. He informed them he had understanding just as they did. He acknowledged God's might, but protested God's treatment of him.

All of Job's friends believed Job had sinned and this was the reason for his punishment. Eliphaz said, "The wicked are punished." Bildad described the fate of sinners. They continued to accuse him and believed he had sinned against God.

Job begged for pity, saying the hand of the Lord had touched him. He said, "I know that my Redeemer liveth, and that He shall stand at the latter day upon the earth. And though after my skin worms destroy this body, yet in my flesh shall I see God." (Job 19:25-26)

Job wanted to take his case directly to God who was the only one capable of vindicating him. He declared he had not sinned and could not understand why God was punishing him. With all the terrible things his friends were saying about him, Job refused to give in to total despair. He maintained his innocence and poured out his heart to God in prayer.

After Job's three friends had finished accusing him, another friend told Job he wanted to speak to him. This was Elihu, who was the youngest, and felt he should wait until last to speak.

Elihu rebuked Job's other friends for failing to answer Job's questions and yet condemned him. He then chastised Job for blaming God for his sufferings. Job had complained that God would not speak to him. Elihu said, "God speaks to people through dreams, pain and through others. You were so distracted by your friends accusations and your suffering you couldn't hear God if He did speak to you."

Elihu told Job and his friends of God's greatness and justice. He said to Job, "Consider the wondrous works of God."

The Lord finally answered Job out of a whirlwind. He told Job of all his mighty acts and asked Job if he could do any of them. Job had said he wanted to argue his case with the Lord. However, when God spoke to Job and asked him questions, Job was speechless.

God did not tell Job why he suffered and did not apologize for His silence. He asked Job questions he could not answer to show Job how inadequate human wisdom is.

Job gained peace by submitting to the Lord. He covered himself in dust and ashes to demonstrate the sorrow in his heart.

God's wrath was kindled against Job's friends as they had not spoken the truth about him. He told them to take a burnt offering to Job and Job would pray for them and He would hear Job's prayer.

After Job prayed for his friends, the Lord restored and doubled his wealth. He also gave Job seven sons and three daughters.

Those who had shunned him during his suffering came to Job to offer sympathy, comfort and encouragement. They also brought money and gold earrings.

After this Job lived one hundred forty years, then he died, being old and full of days.

TWENTY-ONE

ISAIAH

⁓

Isaiah, son of Amoz, was called by god to be a prophet. He was one of the greatest prophets and spoke God's message to Judah for over four decades.

He received visions from God to reveal to the people and prophesied what would happen to Judah and Jerusalem.

The vision he saw, during the reign of Uzziah, Jothem, Ahaz, and Hezekiah, kings of Judah, warned the people they would be judged for their wickedness. They were not living for God and God's wrath would be great against them. Judah's rejection of God had led to meaningless worship and unethical worship. Their future depended on whether the nation would obey or disobey God.

Isaiah told the people, "You have rebelled against God and now you need to alter your lives and cease your disobedience. Also, learn to live good, live by what God has declared to be right. Do not allow anyone to abuse others, defend the right of the fatherless and help the widows."

The country is desolate and your cities burned. Your fields have been destroyed by foreigners. If the Lord had not left a small remnant of people, it would have been like Sodom and Gommorah.

Isaiah told the people, "Hear the Word of the Lord, 'I do not want your burnt offerings or incense. I hate your new moon festivals and appointed feasts. When you pray, I will not hear you.

If you will turn away from your sin and seek judgment, though your sins are as scarlet, they will be washed white as snow. If you rebel, you will be destroyed.

Zion will be pardoned by the Lord's justice, but the rebels and sinners will be consumed.'"

If Judah repented and followed God obediently, the nation could continue to live in their homeland. If they refused to repent and maintained a rebellious attitude toward God, they would lose everything. Their sin is as Sodom and they hide it not. They have

Old Testament Saints and The Messiah

rewarded evil unto themselves. They turned their backs on God who had rescued them from slavery in Egypt and provided for them throughout their history.

Despite Isaiah's preaching the people continued to rebel against God. As a result Judah was conquered by the Babylonian's and Jerusalem was destroyed.

In the last days the mountain of the Lord will be established and all nations will stream to it. The Lord will teach the people His ways so they can live by them. Nations will never fight against each other and they will not train for war again.

Those who are left in Zion and those that remain in Jerusalem will be called holy. He will wash away the filth of the daughters of Zion. There will be a tabernacle to protect the people from the heat, storms and rain.

In a vision, Isaiah saw the Lord sitting upon a throne and angels were standing above Him. Isaiah was very afraid, and said, "Woe is me! For I am undone; because I am a man of unclean lips, and I dwell in the midst of a people of unclean lips; for mine eyes have seen the King, the Lord of Hosts." (Isaiah 6:5)

A seraphim came with a live coal and laid it against Isaiah's lips, and said, "Thine iniquity is taken away and your sin purged."

Isaiah then heard the Lord say, "Who shall I send?" Isaiah said, "Send me." The Lord told Isaiah to go preach the word of God to the people. However, the Lord would close their ears and eyes so they could not see or understand. Isaiah asked the Lord how long he should do this. The Lord said, "Until the cities be wasted without inhabitant and the houses without man and the land be utterly desolate." (Isaiah 6:11)

It was told the house of David that Aram's King Rezin and Israel's King Pekah planned to come, war against them and set a king in their midst. When word reached David's family they were afraid.

The Lord told Isaiah to go to Ahaz, king of Judah, and tell him this would not happen. The Lord said to Ahaz, "Ask thee a sign of the Lord thy God; ask it either in the depth, or in the height above." (Isaiah 7:11)

Ahaz would not ask a sign from the Lord and he would not tempt the Lord. Isaiah said, "The Lord will give you a sign." 'Behold, a virgin shall conceive and bear a son and shall call His name Immanuel. (Isaiah

7:14) Before the child is grown, the land you fear will be forsaken of both her kings.'"

Isaiah prophesied against foreign nations for the benefit of Judah. Judah trusted more in military alliances than in God's protection and worshipped gods of other nations.

Judah depended on Egypt to help them overcome Assyria. When Assyria posed their greatest threat, Egypt reneged on its agreement with Judah. They staked the future of their nation on human power, rather than relying on God and their nation was destroyed.

The Assyrian king had blasphemed God, saying He was powerless as all man made gods whom he could easily defeat. God proved him wrong by destroying the Assyrian army, so they would know the power of God. Sennacherib never invaded Israel again. His sons assassinated him as he worshipped in the temple.

Isaiah announced God would destroy Babylon and Assyria. He declared God's judgment on Philistia, Moab and Damascus. Israel, Cush and Egypt would suffer destruction by God's hand, although Egypt would eventually turn to God in faith.

Syria and Israel trusted in their own power believing they were not accountable to God.

The difficult times of God's judgment accomplished His goal. Israel turned from false gods and returned to the true God.

It shall come to pass that the remnant of Israel and the remnant of Jacob shall return unto the mighty God. The high ones with stature will be hewn down and the haughty shall be humbled.

The spirit of the Lord will rest on the child born of the virgin and He shall judge with righteousness the poor and the meek. He will slay the wicked.

The animals shall feed together and the children can play safely as no one will hurt or destroy on His holy mountain.

The Lord showed Isaiah what would happen to Judah and Jerusalem in the last days. "The mountain of the Lord's house will be established and all nations will flow to it. The Lord will teach His ways and we will walk in His paths. He will judge among the nations and the Lord alone will be exalted in that day. The idols will be destroyed. It shall be well for the righteous, but woe unto the wicked."

Isaiah told Jerusalem her time of servitude was over and her iniquity pardoned. God once again

Old Testament Saints and The Messiah

claimed them for Himself, not because of their righteousness, but out of His grace.

The Lord will come out of His place to punish the inhabitants of the earth for their iniquity. In that day a great trumpet will sound and those who were ready to perish in the land of Assyria and the outcasts in the land of Egypt will worship the Lord in the holy mount in Jerusalem. He that puts his trust in me shall inherit my holy mountain.

The sun, nor moon, will be your light but the Lord shall be an everlasting light and thy God thy glory. Your mourning will be ended. I will create new heavens and a new earth; and the former shall not be remembered. Those who have transgressed against Me shall enter a fire that will not be quenched.

It will be horrible for those who make unjust laws and oppressive regulations. They deprive the poor of justice and take away the rights of needy people. They prey on widows and rob orphans. They will be called to account for these things.

The Lord will punish the king of Assyria for all his boasting and arrogance. Then the remaining few Israelites will no longer depend on those who struck them. They will only depend on the Lord. The remaining few of Jacob will return to the Lord.

Old Testament Saints and The Messiah

The Lord told the people of Zion, "Do not be afraid of the Assyrian's, as My anger will destroy them."

Isaiah had a divine revelation about Babylon. "Israel will be rescued from Babylon and be settled in their own country. The king of Babylon will be brought down for his treatment of the Israelites. The Philistine's and Moabites will be punished. Damascus will no longer be a city.

The Egyptians will cry unto the Lord because of their oppressors and He shall send them a Savior and deliver them."

As Isaiah prophesied, the great Babylonian empire that believed it was invincible, fell to the Persian's. The remnant of Israel who witnessed Babylonian's fall later saw God restore Judah when Cyrus allowed the Jews living in Babylonia to return home.

The Lord reveals to Isaiah what will happen to the Messiah. "He will be despised and rejected by men; a man of sorrows; acquainted with grief. He will carry our sorrows and grief and be wounded for our transgressions. With His stripes we are healed. He will justify many for He shall bear their iniquities."

TWENTY-TWO

JEREMIAH

⚜

Jeremiah, the son of Hilkiah, was a prophet unto the nations. He was called by God to warn Judah of its wickedness.

The Lord told Jeremiah He would give him the words to speak against the kings of Judah, the priests and the people of the land. "They shall fight against you, but they shall not prevail against thee; for I am with thee, saith the Lord, to deliver thee." (Jeremiah 1:19)

The Lord told Jeremiah to tell all the descendents of Jacob and all the families in the nation of Israel, "I brought you out of Egypt into a land of plenty and you defiled the land. The prophets prophesied in the name of Baal. You have abandoned Me, and now I will bring a nation from the north to destroy your harvest, your flocks, herds and your cities. I will not destroy all of you, but will save a few of the faithful. You will wonder why the Lord is doing this and the Lord will say, 'Because you have forsaken Me and served strange gods.'"

The Lord came again to Jeremiah. He told him to go to the people and tell them if they will turn from their backsliding, He will not cause His anger to fall on them for He is merciful and will not keep anger forever. He will give you pastors who will feed you with knowledge and understanding. Jerusalem shall be called the throne of the Lord and all nations shall be gathered to it.

Jeremiah felt defeated, as he had preached and called the people to repentance, but no one listened to him. He stayed faithful to God but believed he had failed. The Lord told him the people would not prevail against him, as He would save and deliver him from them. The Lord did not call Jeremiah to be successful. He called him to preach the word of God and if the people did not listen, it was not Jeremiah's fault.

The Lord told Jeremiah, "Stand in the gates of Jerusalem and tell the king of Judah and all the inhabitants of Jerusalem to amend their ways and observe the Sabbath and the Lord will let you dwell in this place, in the land He gave your fathers, forever. If you do not obey His laws, He will kindle a fire that will not be quenched and it shall devour the palaces of Jerusalem."

The people of Anathoth planned to kill Jeremiah so he could no longer prophecy in the name of the Lord. The Lord told Jeremiah, "I am going to punish them. The young men will die in war, their sons and daughters will die because of the famine and I will bring disaster on the people. It will be a year of punishment and there will be no survivors."

Pashhur, the chief officer of the Lord's temple, put Jeremiah in prison for prophesying. When he released Jeremiah, Jeremiah told him, "The Lord will give all Judah into the hand of Nebuchadnezzar, king of Babylon, and they will be held captive and slain by the sword. The king of Babylon will also be given all your precious things and all the treasures of the king of Judah."

The Lord told Jeremiah to take a scroll and write on it everything He had said about Israel, Judah and all the other nations. The Lord said, "The nation of Judah will hear about all the disasters I plan to bring on them and they will turn from their wicked ways.

If they do this, I will forgive their wickedness and sins."

Jeremiah dictated all the Lord had told him to Baruch. Baruch took it to the officers and then to Jehoiakim, king of Judah. As they read it to the king, he threw it in the fire and burned it.

Jeremiah speaks against the cruel kings of Israel and predicts the coming of a righteous King from David's family tree. He shall be called The Lord our Righteousness. "He shall execute judgment and justice in the earth. In His days Judah will be saved and Israel shall dwell safely. He will lead Israel from all the countries where they were driven and they shall dwell in their own land, be fruitful and increase."

Jeremiah was in prison when Jerusalem was captured. The Babylonians burned the palace, the people's homes and tore down the walls of Jerusalem. They left some of the poor people who had nothing and gave them vineyards and farms.

Jeremiah was released from prison and told if he did not want to go to Babylon he did not have to go. They told him, "The whole land is yours, go wherever you want to go."

The people of Judah asked Jeremiah to pray to the Lord and ask Him where they should go and what they should do. They said whatever the Lord told them they would do. The Lord told Jeremiah to tell the people to stay in the land and He would change His plans about the disaster He had brought upon them. The Lord promised to have compassion for the people.

The people did not do as the Lord commanded. They wanted to go to Egypt where there was no war. The Lord told them if they went to Egypt, He would destroy them with famines, plagues and wars. All of you will die. He will allow King Nebuchadnezzar to defeat Egypt.

The Lord said since Judah had not heard His words, these nations shall serve the king of Babylon for seventy years. When these seventy years are accomplished, God will punish the king of Babylon for their iniquity and will make it a desolation without inhabitants.

TWENTY-THREE

EZEKIEL

Ezekiel was the son of Buzi, who was a priest.

He was taken captive by King Nebuchadnezzar's forces when they captured and conquered the nation of Judah.

The power of the Lord came over Ezekiel, and he saw visions from God. He saw four creatures around the Lord's throne. Then he heard the voice of the Lord telling him, "Go to Israel and speak my words to them. These people are rebellious and if they do not listen, they will know a prophet has been among them." Ezekiel's main message was a call to repentance.

The Lord had Ezekiel bear the punishment Israel and Judah would bear, to show the people what would happen to them if they continued to sin and rebel against Him. The Lord will cut off the bread supply in Jerusalem and ration the water. The people will waste away because of their sins.

The Lord is patient, and is attempting to bring the people back to Himself so He can take care of them. When they do not listen and turn from their evil ways, He allows King Nebuchadnezzar's forces to capture the nation of Judah.

The Lord also had Ezekiel prophesy against false prophets, elders who were practicing idolatry and individual sin. Also, the coming judgment against the Gentile nations. He will send wars, famines, wild animals and plagues to destroy the people and the animals. Some of the people will live.

He was told to prophesy against the mountains of Israel. Their altars would be destroyed, their incense burners smashed and people would be killed when the Lord pronounced His judgment on them. Jerusalem and the temple were doomed to destruction because of the sinfulness and idolatry of the people. Men turned their backs to the temple and worshipped the rising sun. They filled the land with violence, and this provoked the Lord even more.

The Lord sent men throughout Jerusalem to question the people. They were to ask the people if they were against all the disgusting things being done in the city or if they approved of them. Those who were against the disgusting things, had a mark put on their forehead. The Lord sent men out to kill those who did not have the mark.

The Lord told Ezekiel to tell the people of Israel, "The Lord will bring you back from the countries where you are scattered and give you the land of Israel. At that time, you will remove all the detestable things. You will live by My laws and be My people and I will be your God. Those who continue to follow detestable idols will be punished." Ezekiel went to the exiles and told them everything the Lord had shown him.

The Lord passed judgment on the Ammonites as they were happy when the land of Israel was ruined and the nation of Judah was taken into exile. He also passed judgment on Moab, Edom, the Philistines, Sidon, Egypt and Pharaoh.

The ruler of Tyre and all the people were glad when Jerusalem was destroyed, so the Lord sent King Nebuchadnezzar of Babylon to destroy Tyre and all its people.

Ezekiel saw the valley of dry bones. He saw the bones come together at God's command, and God breathed life into them. The Lord told Ezekiel that Israel was like these dry bones. However, the Lord said, "I will gather Israel from all the nations and breath new life into them. They will have a new spirit and live by My laws. You will no longer suffer the disgrace of the nations or hear their insults."

The Lord promised the children of Israel the ruins would be rebuilt, the wasteland plowed and the land will be filled with flocks of people.

Gog, from the land of Magog, with troops and many armies on horses will come from the north to attack the mountains of Israel. The Lord told Ezekiel to prophesy to these troops and tell them, "You will die on the mountains and the armies who are with you. I will feed you to the birds and wild animals, and you will know that I am the Lord, the Holy One of Israel."

TWENTY-FOUR

DANIEL

Nebuchadnezzar, king of Babylon, seized Jerusalem and Jehoiakin, king of Judah. He also took part of the vessels from the house of God and put them in the treasure house of his god.

Daniel and some of his friends were taken captive by King Nebuchadnezzar and carried off to Babylon.

These men's names were Daniel, Hananiah, Mishael and Azariah. However, they were given new names by their captor. They called them Beltshazzar, Shadrach, Mishach and Abednego.

They were told they must change their diet and eat the king's menu. God had instructed these young men as to what to eat and what not to eat. They did not know what to do, as they were afraid if they did not comply with the kings demands, he would torture them to death, as he was a very cruel king.

They chose to honor God and requested they be allowed to eat their diet for ten days and the others eat the king's diet and see who was stronger at the end of the ten days. Daniel and his friends were healthier and stronger, so the others diet was changed to be the same as theirs.

God gave these young men grace to withstand the pressures and they were given high positions in the kingdom.

The king had a dream and called all his wise men to tell him his dream and interpret it for him. They said they could not interpret it unless they knew what the dream was. The king said he had forgotten what the dream was, but it disturbed him. The wise men could not do this and the king issued a decree that all the wise men were to be killed.

When Daniel heard this, he prayed to God for the answer. God granted his request. He asked to be brought before the king to tell him what his dream was and to interpret it for him. Daniel told the king what his dream was and interpreted it for him. Daniel told the king he did not interpret the dream, his God did. The king was so happy he gave Daniel many gifts and made him ruler over the whole province of Babylon. Daniel requested his friends be set over the affairs of the province of Babylon and the king complied.

The king had a huge gold image of himself built. He demanded all the people bow down and worship the image. If they refused they would be thrown into the fiery furnace.

When the king was told Daniel's friends refused to bow down to the image, he was very angry. Daniel's friends told the king their God was able to save them, but if he chose not to save them, they still would not bow down to his image. The king ordered three of his men to tie them up and throw them into the furnace. The fire was so hot that the three men who threw them into the furnace died from the heat.

Then Nebuchadnezzar saw four men walking in the midst of the fire unhurt and he said the fourth man looked like the Son of God. The king called to Shadrach, Meshach and Abednego to come forth from the midst of the fire. All of the people were amazed that these young men had no smell of fire on them, their clothes were not burned and their hair was not singed.

Nebuchadnezzar said, "Blessed be the God of Shadrach, Meshach and Abednego, who hath sent His angel, and delivered his servants that trusted in Him and have changed the kings word, and yielded their bodies, that they might not serve nor worship any god, except their own God." (Daniel 4:28) The king made a decree that anyone who spoke anything amiss against the God of these young men would be cut to pieces.

The king had another dream. Daniel prayed for the Lord to give him an answer. Daniel told the king, "Your kingdom will be taken from you and you will dwell with the beasts of the field and eat grass for seven years, until you admit that the most High rules in the kingdom of men. You will be sent from your palace to eat grass with the wild animals. After seven years you will realize the Lord has power over human kingdoms.

When you realize that heaven rules, your kingdom will be returned to you."

This happened, just as the Lord told Daniel. Finally, the kings mind became clear and he praised God and affirmed that God is the most High and the King of heaven. Nebuchadnezzar's kingdom was restored to him.

Old Testament Saints and The Messiah

King Belshazzar, son of King Nebuchadnezzar, had a huge party. During the party they used the gold and silver goblets which had been taken from God's temple in Jerusalem to drink wine and to toast false gods.

Suddenly a finger wrote a message on the wall. The astrologers and wise men could not interpret it. Daniel asked God to reveal the answer to him. The message was, King Belshazzar would die for his arrogance in using God's gold and silver vessels to toast false god's, and his kingdom would be divided between the Medes and Persians, and king Darius will ascend the throne. King Belshazzar was slain that night and King Darius ascended to his throne.

In an effort to destroy Daniel, his jealous rivals convinced King Darius to establish a decree forbidding anyone from praying to any god or king except King Darius. They knew Daniel would not obey this and they could report him to the king.

When they told the king Daniel was praying to his God, the king was displeased with himself for signing the decree. He wanted to save Daniel, but he could not change the decree.

Daniel was brought before the king and cast in the den of lions. The king said to Daniel, "—The

God whom thou servest continually, He will deliver thee." (Daniel 6:16)

The king could not sleep that night and arose early the next morning and went to the lions' den. He called out to Daniel and Daniel answered him. "My God hath sent His angel, and hath shut the lions' mouths that they have not hurt me; for as much as before Him innocence was found in me; and also before thee, O King, have I done no hurt." (Daniel 6:22)

The king commanded that the men who accused Daniel be brought to the lions' den, along with their wives and children, and be cast into the lions' den.

King Darius then issued another decree to every dominion of his kingdom declaring that Daniel's God is the only true living God.

Daniel has visions of what will happen in the end times, the return of Jesus Christ to set up a new kingdom of God and the reign of Jesus Christ. He is also told of the tribulation period. Jesus will return and those who are written in the Book of Life will be delivered and the dead in Christ will rise to everlasting life.

The Lord told Daniel to close up and seal the words of the scroll until the time of the end. Daniel is

Old Testament Saints and The Messiah

told to wait until the end of the days and he will then receive his allotted inheritance.

TWENTY-FIVE

MINOR PROPHETS

※

These prophets received visions from God showing them what would happen to the people if they did not repent and turn back to God. The prophets told the people what God had revealed to them.

HOSEA

Hosea was the son of Beeri.

He married a prostitute as the Lord had told him. They had children and the Lord compared Hosea's unfaithful wife to Israel.

Israel did not respond to God with faithfulness and love after all the blessings God had bestowed upon them.

The Lord told Hosea what He planned to do to Israel. Hosea told the Israelites God's plan, "Israel and Ephraim will fall in their iniquity and Judah will fall with them."

They still did not repent so the Lord withdrew Himself from them.

The Lord said if they would ask forgiveness for their sins, He would love and restore them. His anger would turn away from them.

JOEL

Joel was the son of Pethuel.

He warned the people that God would send an invasion of locusts and worms in Palestine to destroy their fields and vines for their disobedience to God. He urged the people to repent and pray that God would restore the land. Joel told the people that God loved them and He would restore the land if they would repent and return to Him.

He warned the people that the day of the Lord was near and there would be woe and judgment. The people would cry out because there would be no food. There will be sorrow and mourning because of the people's sins. God loves His people too much to allow them to continue in sin without consequences.

In the day of the Lord, all who call on the name of the Lord shall be delivered. The day of the Lord is near, but the Lord will be the hope of His people and the strength of the children of Israel.

Joel told the people to repent and God would save them from their enemies. He said all nations will be judged and in the last days, Jerusalem will be holy and no foreigners will invade her. Egypt will be desolate and Edom will be a desert waste because of the violence done to the people of Judah.

AMOS

Amos was a shepherd but was called by God to prophesy to Israel.

The Lord told Amos how He would punish Israel for all their sins. They had turned away from God, were cruel to the poor and lived selfishly.

In a vision, Amos saw that the day of doom was close. He warned the people to return to God and live by His commandments and prepare to meet God.

The Lord said He would destroy Israel from the face of the earth, but not the house of Jacob.

Amos said the day will come when the Lord will bring back His exiled people Israel to rebuild the city and plant the vineyards.

OBADIAH

Obadiah prophesied against the nation of Edom. He said they would be destroyed as they had invaded Jerusalem, and because of Esau's violence against his brother Jacob. He watched as strangers carried his forces away and foreigners entered his gates. Esau was one of them.

Esau rejoiced over the children of Judah in their day of destruction. He did so many cruel things that the Lord warned him the things he had done would return to his own head. The Edomites will be humiliated, disgraced and destroyed forever as a nation.

There will be no survivors from the house of Esau. The kingdom will be the Lord's.

JONAH

The Lord sent Jonah to Nineveh to warn the people to repent of their evil ways or He would destroy them.

Jonah ran from the Lord and got on a ship to Tarshish.

The Lord sent a great storm. The sailors were frightened as the sea kept getting rougher. Jonah knew he was the reason the Lord sent the storm, so he told the sailors to throw him overboard and the storm would cease. They threw him overboard and the sea became calm.

The Lord sent a great fish to swallow Jonah. Jonah was inside the fish three days and three nights. He prayed to the Lord to save him, and promised he would go to Nineveh to warn the people. The fish spit him out onto dry ground.

He did as the Lord had commanded and warned the people of Nineveh to repent within forty days or the Lord would overturn Nineveh. They believed God and turned from their evil ways. The king and his nobles demanded everyone to call on God so they would not perish.

When God saw the people had repented and turned from their evil ways, He had compassion and did not destroy them as He had threatened.

MICAH

Micah warned Jerusalem and Samaria if the rulers, prophets and priests continued to sin, they would face God's judgment. The Lord said Zion would be plowed like a field and Jerusalem will become a heap of rubble.

Jerusalem declared its destruction resulted from its sin and not from the might of the Babylonian army.

Their enemies asked, "Where is the Lord your God?" Jerusalem's restoration would demonstrate God's reality. The enemy who gloated over Jerusalem's fall will fall and be trampled underfoot.

The rebuilding of the walls would indicate God's forgiveness of His people. Micah's prophecy came true when Nehemiah succeeded in leading the people to rebuild Jerusalem's walls.

However, in the last days, the house of the Lord will be established and many people and nations will come to the mountain of the Lord to the house of God.

Micah also prophesied that out of Bethlehem will come one who will be ruler over Israel.

NAHUM

Nahum warned the people of Nineveh of the Lord's anger. Nineveh was the capital of Assyria and they had conquered many nations. They were cruel to the people. Nahum predicted the siege and destruction of Nineveh and the end of the kingdom of Assyria.

Judah was told to observe their religious feasts as the Assyrian's would never again threaten Jerusalem.

HABAKKUK

Habakkuk had a conversation with God about the violence of the land, of the city and all who live there. He asked the Lord why He was letting these wicked people prosper.

The Lord told Habakkuk to write on a tablet for all to see what will happen at the appointed time. They will all be afraid as the wicked will be punished. God will raise up the Chaldeans to deal with Judah's sinful rebellion.

Habakkuk praised the Lord. The God of his salvation.

ZEPHANIAH

He was the son of Cushi. He warned the people that the day of the Lord would bring judgment on Judah and Jerusalem. He urged the people to return to God and ask forgiveness for their wicked ways. The Lord said if they would obey His commandments He would take away their punishment and turn their enemies away.

In the last days, the remnant of Israel shall repent. The Lord will take away their judgments and they shall not see evil again.

Jerusalem will be saved and God will gather all who are sorrowful and undo those who afflict them.

HAGGAI

The people of Judah were living a life of ease and had their priorities out of order. Instead of putting God first, they had forgotten Him as they focused on their own lives. God told the people to change their ways of life.

The word of the Lord came to Haggai that it was time to rebuild the temple. Zerubbabel, the governor of Judah, and Joshua, the high priest, and all the people obeyed the Lord and rebuilt the temple.

The temple was rebuilt under the leadership of Zerubbabel and Joshua.

When the people neglected God, there was judgment against them. However, when they turned to God and obeyed His commandments, He blessed them.

The Lord told Haggai to tell Zerubbabel, the governor of Judah, that He will overthrow the throne of the kingdoms and destroy the strengths of the kingdoms of the heathens and will make Zerubbabel a signet.

ZECHARIAH

Zechariah was the son of Berechiah.

The Lord was very displeased with Judah's ancestors and told Zechariah to tell the people to return to Him and He would turn unto the people and save them from their enemies.

Zechariah warned the people they were to listen to God's message through the prophets and keep a close relationship with God.

The angel of the Lord came to Zechariah and said, "The Lord will return to Jerusalem with mercies. The house of the Lord will be built in Jerusalem and He will comfort Zion. Jerusalem will be called a city of truth, and the mountain of the Lord of hosts, the holy mountain."

The angel of the Lord is revealing to Zechariah what will happen in the world in the last days when the Messiah returns. The Lord will bring a curse on the whole earth on the evildoers and salvation for His people.

MALACHI

Malachi warned the Israelites they must turn to God and honor Him or there would be judgment.

They asked God what they had done to anger Him.

God told them, "The priests have not honored My name. The teachings do not preserve knowledge, but show partiality in matters of the law. Judah has desecrated the sanctuary the Lord loves by marrying daughters of foreign gods. You have robbed God of tithes and offerings. The day of the Lord is coming and the arrogant and evildoer will be stubble, but those who revere My name and live by the law of Moses will be blessed."

TWENTY-SIX

THE MESSIAH

⚜

Thousands of years before the Messiah was born, the Lord revealed to the Old Testament prophets He would send the Messiah to teach, heal and save the people.

Moses: "Rejoice O ye nations, with His people, for He will avenge the blood of His servants and will render vengeance to His adversaries, and will be merciful unto His land and to His people." (Deuteronomy 32:43)

Isaiah: "Therefore the Lord Himself shall give you a sign; Behold, a virgin shall conceive, and bear a son, and shall call His name Immanuel." (Isaiah 7:14)

Jeremiah: "Behold, the days are come, saith the Lord, that I will raise unto David a righteous Branch, and a King shall reign and prosper, and shall execute judgment and justice in the earth. In His days Judah shall be saved, and Israel shall dwell safely: and this is His name whereby He shall be called, The Lord our Righteousness." (Jeremiah 23:5-6)

Micah: "But thou, Bethlehem Ephratah, though thou be little among the thousands of Judah, yet out of thee shall He come forth unto Me that is to be the ruler of Israel; whose goings forth have been from old to everlasting." (Micah 5:2)

Zechariah: "Hear now, O Joshua the high priest, thou, and thou fellows that sit before thee: for they are men wondered at; for, behold, I will bring forth My Servant the Branch." (Zechariah 3:8)

Malachi: "Behold I will send My messenger, and He shall prepare the way before Me: and the Lord whom ye seek, shall suddenly come to His temple, even the messenger of the covenant, whom you delight in: Behold, He shall come, saith the Lord of Hosts." (Malachi 3:1)

The Lord wanted the people to know Jesus would avenge the blood of His servants, and render vengeance to His adversaries. He said, "He will be merciful unto His land and His people."

Jesus' mother, Mary, was espoused to Joseph. Before they came together, Mary was found with child of the Holy Ghost. Joseph did not want to embarrass Mary, but he thought about putting her away secretly. An angel of the Lord appeared to him in a dream, telling him his wife was conceived by the Holy Ghost, and will bring forth a son and you will name Him Jesus, for He shall save His people from their sins.

Joseph did as the angel of the Lord told him, and took his wife, Mary, but knew her not until after the birth of her son.

Joseph went to Bethlehem to be registered with Mary. While they were there Jesus was born and was laid in a manger, as there was no room for them at the Inn.

Herod, the king, and all Jerusalem were troubled when they heard Jesus was born. King Herod called all the chief priests and scribes of the people together and asked where Christ was born. They told him Jesus was born in Bethlehem of Judea.

King Herod sent three wise men to find Jesus. They followed the star and when they came to where Jesus and His mother were, they fell down and worshipped Him. They brought many gifts to Jesus;

gold, frankincense and myrrh. The wise men were warned by God that they should not return to Herod, and they went into their own country another way.

The angel of the Lord came to Joseph and told him to take Jesus and his mother and go to Egypt, as Herod would seek to destroy the child. Joseph went by night to Egypt and stayed there until the death of Herod.

When Herod saw he was mocked by the wise men, he was very angry. He had all the male children, two years of age and under, slain in Bethlehem and the coasts thereof.

After Herod died, an angel of the Lord appeared to Joseph in a dream in Egypt. He told Joseph to take the child and His mother to Israel. When Joseph found Herod's son, Archelaus, was reigning in Judea, he was afraid and went to Nazareth.

John the Baptist went throughout the wilderness of Judea preaching, saying, "Repent for the kingdom of heaven is at hand." All Jerusalem and Judea and the region around the Jordan came to be baptized, confessing their sins. Then Jesus came from Galilee to Jordan to be baptized by John the Baptist. As Jesus came up out of the water, the Spirit of God descended like a dove and lighted upon him, and lo a voice from

Old Testament Saints and The Messiah

heaven saying, "This is My beloved Son, in whom I am well pleased." (Matthew 3:17)

Then Jesus was led by the Spirit to the wilderness to be tempted by the devil. He fasted for forty days and forty nights and was very hungry. The devil tempted him with many promises, but Jesus refused to do what the devil asked. The devil finally left Him and angels of the Lord came and ministered unto Him.

Jesus heard that John had been cast into prison, and He left Nazareth and dwelt in Capernaum.

Jesus began to preach and tell the people to repent, as the kingdom of heaven was at hand. He called Peter, Andrew, James and John to follow Him. He went throughout Galilee teaching in the synagogues and preaching the gospel of the kingdom. He healed all manner of sickness and disease among the people. Some of the people were healed by just touching the hem of His robe.

Great multitudes followed from Galilee, Decapolis, Jerusalem, Judea and from beyond Jordan.

When Jesus saw the multitude of people, He went up on a mountain and preached the famous sermon,

"The Sermon on the Mount", telling the people what they must do to live in God's will.

Some of His teachings are as follows: He told the people, "Do not pray in vain repetitions as the heathens do, as they are praying to be heard by men. When you pray, go into a quiet place and pray to your Heavenly Father in secret.

Do not store up treasures on earth that will be destroyed, but store up treasures in heaven, as where your treasures are, there your heart will be also.

Enter through the narrow gate as this road leads to life. The wide gate is the road that leads to destruction."

"Ask and it shall be given you, seek and ye shall find, knock and it shall be opened unto you." (Matthew 7:7)

Jesus demonstrated his authority over every realm of human struggle. There was nothing He could not do. He healed the sick, walked on water, calmed the storm and turned water into wine. He fed multitudes on a few loaves of bread and a few fishes.

Jesus and His disciples went to Matthew's house for dinner. There were publicans and sinners sitting with them. The Pharisees began to question Jesus' disciples, asking why Jesus was eating with them.

Old Testament Saints and The Messiah

Jesus heard them and said, "They that be whole need not a physician, but they that are sick." (Matthew 9:12)

Jesus called His twelve disciples, Simon (Peter), Andrew, James (The son of Zebedee), John, Phillip, Bartholomew, Thomas, Matthew, James (The son of Alphaeus), Lebbaeus (whose surname is Thaddeus), Simon and Judas Iscariot, and gave them authority to drive out evil spirits, to heal every disease and sickness. He told them to go to the lost sheep of Israel and preach, saying, "The kingdom of heaven is at hand." (Matthew 10:7)

When Jesus finished commanding His disciples, He went into the cities to preach and teach. The cities where most of His mighty work was done, repented not. Jesus said, "Woe unto you Chorazin, Bethsaida, and Capernaum, it shall be more tolerable for the land of Sodom in the day of judgment, than for you."

Jesus began telling His disciples how He must suffer many things from the elders, chief priests and scribes. He told them He must die, but would be raised from the dead on the third day. He said at the end of this world, He will send His angels and they shall gather out of His kingdom all who offend and do iniquity. They will be cast into the furnace of fire. The righteous will shine forth as the sun in the kingdom of our Father.

The Pharisee's held council against Jesus as to how they might destroy Him.

When Jesus saw people buying and selling in the temple, He went in and drove out all who were buying and selling there. He turned over tables of the moneychangers and told them, "My house shall be called a house of prayer; but ye have made it a den of thieves." (Matthew 21:13)

As Jesus departed from the temple, the disciples came to Him, to show Him the buildings of the temple. Jesus said, "There shall not be left here one stone upon another that shall not be thrown down." (Matthew 24:2)

Jesus and his disciples went up to the Mount of Olives. He told His disciples what would happen at the end of the age. His disciples asked when this would be and if there would be a sign of Jesus coming and the end of the world.

Jesus said, "Many shall come in My name. You will hear of wars and rumors of wars, nation shall rise against nation, and kingdom against kingdom. There shall be famines, pestilences and earthquakes in many places. All these are the beginning of sorrows. Many false christs and false prophets shall rise and deceive the people by showing great signs and wonders. Iniquity shall abound and the love of many will grow cold. He that endures unto the end shall be saved. The gospel of the kingdom shall be preached in all the world, then the end shall come. Immediately after the tribulation, the sun will be darkened, the moon shall not give light, the stars will fall from heaven and the powers of heaven shaken. Then you shall see the Son of Man coming in the clouds of heaven with power and great glory. Angels will sound their trumpet and they will gather His children from the four winds, from one end of heaven to the other. Heaven and earth shall pass away. But the day and hour no man knows, only My Father in heaven knows."

The Son of man shall come in His glory with the holy angels. He shall sit upon the throne of His glory. All nations shall be gathered before Him and He shall divide the sheep from the goats, with the sheep on His right hand and the goats on His left.

To those on His right hand, He said, "Inherit the kingdom prepared for you from the foundation of the world." (Matthew 25:34)

To those on His left, He said, "Depart from Me, ye cursed, into the everlasting fire, prepared for the devil and his angels." (Matthew 25:41)

After Jesus finished speaking to His disciples, He told them He had been betrayed and would be crucified.

The chief priests, the scribes and the elders of the people assembled together at the palace of the high priest, who was Caiaphas, and made plans to kill Jesus.

Judas Iscariot, one of the twelve disciples, went to the chief priests and asked what they would give him if he would deliver Jesus to them. They paid him thirty pieces of silver. From that time Judas waited for an opportunity to betray Jesus.

Jesus told His disciples at the Passover feast that Judas Iscariot would betray Him and Peter would deny Him.

Jesus predicted His death and focused on preparing His close followers for what lay ahead. He said, "They shall deliver Me to the Gentiles, who will mock, scourge and crucify Me and the third day I shall rise again. After I have risen again, I will go before you into Galilee."

Then Jesus and his disciples went to Gethsemane. Three times Jesus told his disciples to keep watch as He prayed. Each time they fell asleep. Jesus prayed, "O My Father, if this cup may not pass away from Me, except I drink it, thy will be done." (Matthew 26:42)

Judas and a great multitude of chief priests and elders of the people came with swords and staves. Judas told them whomever he kissed would be Jesus and for them to take Him. All this was done that the scriptures of the prophets might be fulfilled. Then all the disciples forsook Him, and fled. (Matthew 26:56)

Jesus was led away to Caiaphas, the high priest, where the scribes and the elders were assembled.

The high priest accused Jesus of blasphemy. He asked Jesus, "Tell us whether you are the Christ, the Son of God?"

Jesus answered, "Thou hast said; nevertheless, I say unto you, hereafter, shall ye see the Son of man sitting on the right hand of power, and coming in the clouds of heaven." (Matthew 26:64)

The high priest accused Him of blasphemy. Everyone said, "He is guilty, crucify Him." They spit in His face, and hit Him with the palms of their hands. The next morning they bound Him and led Him away to Pontius Pilate, the governor.

When Judas saw Jesus was condemned, he took the thirty pieces of silver and threw them into the temple, went and hanged himself.

The chief priests took the thirty pieces of silver and bought the potter's field in which to bury strangers.

It was the custom to release a prisoner on the day of the feast. Pilate asked who they wanted released. All of them said, "Release Barabbas and crucify Jesus." Pilate saw he could not prevail. He took water and washed his hands before the multitude and said, "I am innocent of the blood of this just person." (Matthew 27:24)

The soldiers of the governor took Jesus into the common hall, stripped Him and put a scarlet robe on Him. They put a crown of thorns on His head and took a reed and hit Him on the head. After they had mocked Him, they took the robe off, put His clothes back on Him and led Him away to be crucified.

Simon, a man from Cyrene, helped Jesus carry His cross. They came to Golgatha and while He hang on the cross they offered Him vinegar to drink. He would not drink it.

After He was crucified, they cast lots for His garments. There were two thieves crucified with Him. One on the right and one on the left.

From the sixth hour until the ninth hour there was darkness over all the land. About the ninth hour Jesus cried out, "My God, My God, why hast thou forsaken Me?" He then died and the temple was destroyed from the top to the bottom. The earth quaked and graves were opened. Many of the saints who slept there arose and came out of the graves after Jesus' resurrection and went into the city where they were seen by many.

When the centurion, and those who were with him watching Jesus, saw the earthquake and those things which were done, they said, "Truly this was the Son of God."

A rich man from Arimathaea, named Joseph, asked Pilate for Jesus' body. He took him and buried Him in a tomb he had built for himself. He rolled a great stone to the door of the tomb and departed. The chief priests and Pharisees sealed the stone at the entrance of the tomb. They sat and watched to make sure Jesus' disciples did not come and steal His body.

On the first day of the week there was a great earthquake, for the angel of the lord descended from heaven and rolled back the stone from the tomb. The angel sat on the stone, the keepers were afraid and became as dead men.

Mary Magdelene and another Mary came to the tomb and the angel told them, "He is not here, He has risen." He told the women to go tell the disciples that Jesus had risen and is going to Galilee. As they left, they met Jesus and He told them to tell His disciples to meet Him in Galilee.

When the disciples met Jesus, He told them, "All power has been given to Me in heaven and in earth. Go ye therefore and teach all nations, baptizing them in the name of the Father, and of the Son, and of the Holy Ghost, teaching them to observe all things whatsoever I have commanded you, and lo, I am with you always, even unto the end of the world." (Matthew 28:18-20)

They watched as Jesus was taken up into heaven.

While John was in prison on the island of Patmos, Jesus sent His angel to tell him what must happen on earth before the end of time.

He told John to write in a book what he was about to see and the things which are and the things which shall be hereafter.

Blessed is he that readeth, and they that hear the words of this prophecy, and keep those things which are written therein; for the time is at hand. (Revelation 1:1-3)

Write to the seven churches of Asia, which are, Ephesus, Smyrna, Pergamos, Thyatira, Sardis, Philadelphia and Laodicea. Jesus warned all the churches, "Repent and overcome that you may eat from the tree of life, which is in the paradise of God. He that overcometh shall not be hurt of the second death. They will sit with Me in My throne, even as I also overcame and am sitting with My Father in His throne."

John looked and a door was opened in heaven. A voice said to him, "Come look and I will show you things which must be hereafter." John was immediately in the spirit.

There was a scroll written inside and on the back, sealed with seven seals. In the midst of the throne were many angels, the four living creatures, the elders and the number of them were ten thousand times ten thousand and thousands of thousands. They were saying, "Blessing, honor, glory and power be unto Him that sits on the throne, and with the Lamb forever and ever."

As Jesus opened each seal, men were sent out to conquer, take peace from the earth, cause famines and pestilences, and one fourth of the people on earth would be killed. When the sixth seal was broken, there was a great earthquake, the sun became dark and the moon became as blood. The people hid in the rocks of the mountains as they were so afraid and said, "The wrath of God has come upon the earth."

The seal of God was placed on 144,000 children of Israel, so they would not be harmed.

After this I beheld a great multitude which no man could number from all nations, peoples and tongues standing before the throne. They were saying in a loud voice, "Salvation to our God who sits on the throne and unto the Lamb." These were the ones who came out of Great Tribulation, washed their robes and made them white in the blood of the Lamb. They are before the throne, and serve Him day and night in His temple. He that sits on the throne shall dwell among them. They will not hunger or thirst anymore for the Lamb will feed them and wipe every tear from their eyes.

When the seventh seal was broken, there were seven trumpets. As each was sounded, one third of the trees and grass burned; a mountain was thrown into the sea; one third of the sea turned into blood; one third of the rivers and springs became wormwood; one third of the sun, moon and stars were struck and one third of day and night were darkened.

Locusts came upon the earth from the bottomless pit. They were given the power to harm all men who did not have the seal of God on their foreheads. They were not to kill the people, but only torture them.

Four angels were released to kill one third of mankind. The rest of mankind did not repent. They still worshipped demons and idols. They did not repent of their murders, thefts and sexual immorality.

The Lord then sent two witnesses to prophecy one thousand two hundred sixty days. When they finish their testimony, the beast will make war against them. They will be killed and lay in the street three and one half days. Then they will rise to their feet and ascend into heaven. At this time, there will be a great earthquake, and one tenth of the city of Babylon will fall and seven thousand men killed.

War broke out in heaven. Michael and his angels fought the devil and his angels. The devil and his angels were cast out of heaven.

The beast appeared and the devil gave him all his power, his throne and great authority.

The people worshipped the beast. He spoke great things and blasphemies. He was given authority to continue forty two months. He was granted power to make war with the saints and to overcome them. Everyone on earth will worship him except those written in the Lamb's Book of Life.

Another beast appeared. He performs great signs and makes fire come down from heaven. He had an image of the beast made and was granted power to give breath to the image of the beast so the image could speak. The people were told they would be killed if they did not bow down to the image and worship it. Those who refused were beheaded.

No one could buy or sell if they did not have the mark of the beast or the number of his name on their hand or forehead.

A Lamb stood on Mt. Sion and 144,000 people with God's mark on their forehead were redeemed from the earth.

Another angel in the midst of heaven, preached the gospel to all who were on the earth, telling them to fear God and give glory to Him, as His hour of judgment has come.

Another angel came to announce that Babylon had fallen.

A third angel said anyone who took the mark of the beast, shall receive the wrath of God and be tormented with fire and brimstone forever and ever.

John saw all the saints standing around the throne who had gotten the victory over the beast, over his image and his mark. They are the ones who keep the commandments of God and faith in Jesus. They were singing the song of Moses, the servant of God.

John then saw the temple of the tabernacle in heaven opened. Seven angels came out with seven plagues. They were given seven gold vials full of the wrath of God. They were sent to pour out the wrath of God on the earth.

The spirits of the devils came out of the dragon, the beast and the false prophet, to gather the kings of the earth and the whole world to gather them to the battle of that great day of God almighty. The people were gathered together in a place called Armageddon. A great voice out of the temple of heaven, from the throne, saying, "It is done." There were voices, thunders, lightning and a great earthquake and the great city of Babylon was divided into three parts. Every island fell away and the mountains were not found. Large hail fell from heaven on the people.

"I saw heaven opened and behold a white horse; and He that sat on him was called Faithful and True, and in righteousness He doth judge and make war." (Revelation 19:11)

The armies which were in heaven followed Him on white horses. Out of His mouth came a sharp sword to smite the nations. An angel called to the fowls of the air to come together to the supper of the great God, that they could eat the flesh of kings, mighty men and horses.

The beast, false prophet, the kings of the earth and their armies, gathered together to make war against the Lord.

The beast, prophet and those who took the mark of the beast, were cast into the lake of fire. The rest of the people were killed by the sword and left for the fowls of the air to eat their flesh.

An angel came down from heaven with a chain. The devil was bound for a thousand years.

Old Testament Saints and The Messiah

The souls who were beheaded for their witness of Jesus, did not receive the mark of the beast and did not worship him, lived and reigned with Christ for a thousand years. This was the first resurrection. The rest of the dead did not live until after the thousand years.

After the thousand years, satan will be released and will deceive the nations in the four quarters of the earth. When he comes to the camp of the saints, fire will come down from God out of heaven and devour him. Then satan will be cast into the lake of fire to be tormented forever and ever.

John then saw a great white throne. The sea gave up the dead and hell delivered up the dead and they were judged. Death and hell were cast into the lake of fire. This was the second death.

He then saw a new heaven and a new earth, as the first heaven and earth had passed away and there was no more sea. John saw the new Jerusalem coming down from heaven.

A great voice from heaven said, "Behold the Tabernacle of God is with men, and He will dwell with them, and they shall be His people, and God Himself will be with them and will be their God." (Revelation 21:3)

God will wipe away all tears and there shall be no more death, sorrow, crying or pain.

One of the angels came to John and he was carried away in the spirit. The angel showed John the great city, the Holy Jerusalem descending out of heaven from God.

"Blessed are they that do His commandments, that they may have the right to the tree of life, and may enter in through the gates into the city." (Revelation 22:14)

QUESTIONS FOR INDIVIDUAL OR GROUP STUDIES

❦

Chapter One:

    Who created the heaven and the earth?

    What else did He create?

    How did God make man?

    How was woman made?

    Who did God put in the garden of Eden?

    Did they disobey God?

    Who told them to disobey God?

    What did they do to disobey God?

    Were they punished?

    How were they punished?

    What does God tell man to do when he is joined to a wife?

Who brought sin into the world?
What did Cain do to Abel, and why?

Chapter Two:
Why did God send a flood to destroy the earth?
Who did God choose to build the ark?
How long did it take to build the ark?
Who went into the ark to be saved?
How long did it rain?
How long were the flood waters on the earth?
What was God's promise after the flood?
How old was Noah when he died?

Chapter Three:
What was Abraham's name before the Lord changed it?
Who was Abraham's wife?
Did God change her name?
What name did God give her?
What did God tell Abraham to do?
Where did Abraham live after he left Ur?
What did God promise Abraham?
Did Abraham obey Him?
What did Sarah do to Haggar, and why?

How old were Abraham and Sarah when their son was born?

What was their son's name?

What happened to Lot's wife?

What did Abraham tell his wife to tell Pharaoh?

What did he tell her to tell Abimelech?

Who was Abraham's second wife?

When Abraham was old, what did he tell his senior servant to do?

Chapter Four:

Who was Isaac's wife?

Did they have children?

What were the children's names?

Which of the children did Isaac love most?

Which of the children did Rebekah love more?

Who sold their birthright?

To whom did he sell it?

Which son stole the blessing?

Who did Jacob marry?

What task did he have to perform to get his wife?

How did Laban deceive Jacob?

What name did God give Jacob?

How many sons did Jacob have?

What were their names?

What happened to Jacob's daughter, Dinah?

What did her brothers do when they heard what Shechem had done?

Chapter Five:

Who were Judah's parents?

What did his brothers plan to do with Joseph?

Did Judah agree?

Who did Judah marry?

What were his son's names?

What did Judah's father tell him before his death?

Who went up against the Canaanites to fight them?

What did the Lord say He would do for the house of Israel and Judah in the last days?

Chapter Six:

Why did Jacob love Joseph more than any of his sons?

What did Joseph's brothers do to him?

What did they tell their father when Joseph did not return home with them?

How did God bless Joseph?

Old Testament Saints and The Messiah

What was the dream Joseph interpreted for Pharaoh?

Did it come to pass?

If so, what happened?

What did Pharaoh do for Joseph?

Did Joseph ever see his brothers again?

Were the brothers sad about what they had done to Joseph?

How did Joseph react to his brothers?

Did Joseph see his father again?

What were the names of Joseph's sons?

Which son got the first blessing from Jacob?

What was Jacob's reason for blessing this son first?

Chapter Seven:

When the children of Israel came to Egypt what did they do?

Did this anger Pharaoh?

What did Pharaoh tell his people?

Who found Moses in the ark of bulrushes?

Who raised him?

Why did Pharaoh hate Moses?

How did the children of Israel escape from Egypt?

Old Testament Saints and The Messiah

What does the Passover mean?

What happened during the Passover?

How long were the children of Israel in Egypt?

What miracles did God perform to get Pharaoh to let the people go?

Name several things God did to the Egyptians?

When Moses met God on the mount, how long was he gone?

What did Aaron do when Moses did not return for quite some time?

How did the children of Israel cross the sea?

Did Pharaoh and his army cross the sea safely?

Moses sent men to spy out the land of Canaan. How long were they gone?

How did the Lord punish the children of Israel because of their complaints?

Which men did God save from this punishment?

How did God punish Moses and Aaron for not hallowing His name at the waters of Meribah?

Did Moses or Aaron get to lead the children of Israel into the land of Canaan?

Who led the children of Israel into the land of Canaan?

Chapter Eight:
> What did the Lord allow Joshua to do?
>
> What did the Lord tell the children of Israel to do to cause the walls of Jericho to fall down?
>
> Did the children of Israel obey the Lord when He told them not to take any of the accursed things?
>
> What did God tell them to do to the person who took the accursed things?
>
> Who divided the land to the children of Israel?
>
> After the children of Israel received their land, did they serve the Lord all the days Joshua lived?
>
> How old was Joshua when he died?

Chapter Nine:
> Did Gideon believe it was the Lord speaking to him?
>
> What did he ask the Lord to do?
>
> What did the Lord tell Gideon to do?
>
> When the people wanted to kill Gideon, what did his father tell them?
>
> What did the Lord do to the Midianites?
>
> Who refused to give Gideon and his men food?

Did Gideon punish those who refused to give them food?

Did the Israelites live in peace during Gideon's life?

What happened to the Israelites after Gideon died?

Chapter Ten:

Who was Samson's mother?

What did Samson do when he passed the lion he had killed?

What did Samson ask his guests to do?

After Samson left his wife, who did her father give her to?

Samson went back to see his wife and her father would not let him see her. What did Samson do?

What did the Philistines do to Samson's wife and her father?

How did Samson kill 1000 men?

Who did Samson reveal where his strength was from?

After this, what happened to Samson?

How did Samson die?

Chapter Eleven:
> Who was the first Prophet?
>
> Who was the first king of Israel?
>
> What promise did Hannah make to God?
>
> Did she keep her promise?
>
> What did the Lord tell Samuel He was going to do to Eli?
>
> What did the Lord tell Samuel to tell the house of Israel?
>
> When Samuel was old, what did they ask Samuel to do?
>
> Who did the Lord tell Samuel to choose to reign over His people?
>
> What did the king do to anger the Lord?
>
> Who did the Lord choose to take the kings place?

Chapter Twelve:
> Who was the champion in the camp of the Philistines?
>
> Why did they call him a champion?
>
> Who fought and killed the champion?
>
> How did he kill the champion?
>
> Why did Saul hate David and try to kill him?
>
> Who did David marry first?

Old Testament Saints and The Messiah

What did David do when he had the chance to kill Saul?

What reviled David when he asked for bread and water for his men?

Who did he ask for bread and water for his men?

What did this mans wife do when she heard her husband refused to give them bread and water?

When she told her husband what she had done, what was her husband's reaction?

What was the name of this mans wife?

What happened to her husband?

What happened to his wife after he died?

What did Saul do when he saw the army of the Philistines?

What did Samuel tell Saul the Lord would do to him when he fought the Philistines?

Did Saul and his three sons die in this battle?

How did Saul die?

Can you name Saul's sons?

How long was David king in Hebron over the house of Judah?

Where was David king after he left Hebron?

Old Testament Saints and The Messiah

What happened when David lay with Bathsheba, the wife of Uriah?
What did David do to Uriah?
How did God punish David and Bathsheba?
Did David and Bathsheba have another son?
What was his name?
What did God tell David his son would do for him?

When King David was old and about to die, what did Bathsheba ask him to do?
How many years did David reign over Israel?

Chapter Thirteen:
Who was anointed king over Israel when King David was about to die?
Who did Solomon marry?
What did Solomon ask for from the Lord?
Was the Lord pleased with his request?
What did the Lord give Solomon?
Who built the house of the Lord?
Who furnished the cedar and fir? What did he receive in return?
How long did it take Solomon to build the house of the Lord?

How long did it take him to build his house?

What was the queen's name who visited Solomon?

Did Solomon disobey God before he died?

What did he do?

How many wives, princesses and concubines did Solomon have?

What did the Lord tell Solomon He would do when Solomon disobeyed Him?

How long did Solomon reign over Israel?

After he died, who reigned in his place?

Chapter Fourteen:

Who was the worst of all kings?

Who did he marry?

Did he worship God?

Where did the Lord send Elijah when He cut off the rains for several years?

After the brook dried up, where did the Lord send Elijah?

What did Elijah tell the widow?

Did the widow's son survive after Elijah prayed for him?

What did Jezebel do to the prophets of the Lord?

How did Obadiah save some of the prophets?

Old Testament Saints and The Messiah

How did Elijah prove God was the God of Israel?

What did the people do when he proved this?

What happened to the Baal prophets?

What did Jezebel do when she heard what Elijah had done to the Baal prophets?

What did Jezebel do to Naboth when he refused to sell his vineyard to Ahab?

What did the Lord do to Ahab for his evil act?

How did Elijah and Elisha cross the Jordan river?

Did Elijah die?

Chapter Fifteen:

Who anointed Elisha as a prophet?

When Elijah asked Elisha what he could do for him, what did he ask for?

What advice did Elisha give the lady who told him a creditor was coming to take her two sons as bondmen?

What did the lady and her husband do for Elisha?

What did Elisha do for them, out of gratitude?

Naaman was a leper. What did Elisha tell him to do to be healed?

Naaman offered Elisha a blessing and Elisha would not take it. What happened after Naaman left Elisha?

What did Elisha tell Gehazi would happen to him?

How long was Elisha a prophet in Israel?

Chapter Sixteen:

Did Hezekiah do as the Lord commanded when he became king?

What did he do?

What did the Lord do to the king of Assyria?

When Hezekiah became sick, what did the Lord tell him?

What did Isaiah say would happen after Hezekiah showed the Babylonian's everything in his treasury and in his palace?

After Hezekiah died, who took his place as king?

Did he follow God's commands?

What did the Lord do to Judah and Jerusalem?

Chapter Seventeen:

What did King Cyrus tell the people to do?

- Who took the vessels from the house of the Lord when he took the children of Israel into bondage?
- Did the people object to the Jews rebuilding the temple and the walls?
- What did the workers tell Darius, king of Persia, to do?
- Did Darius allow the workers to continue their work?
- What complaint was brought to Ezra against the people, priests and Levites?
- Was Ezra disturbed by this news and what did he tell the people?
- What did those who had transgressed against God do?

Chapter Eighteen:
- What was Nehemiah's job?
- Was Nehemiah sad when he heard what had happened in Jerusalem?
- What did he do?
- Who tried to stop the building of the walls?
- What did Nehemiah's enemies try to get him to do?

Old Testament Saints and The Messiah

How long did it take to build the walls and gates in Jerusalem?

After the walls were complete, what did Ezra do?

How did they determine who would live in Jerusalem?

What did the book of Moses say about the Ammonite's and the Moabite's?

After Eliasheb allowed Tobiah to move into the house of the Lord, what did Nehemiah do?

Tell some of the things that happened while Nehemiah went to see the king, and what did Nehemiah do about it?

Chapter Nineteen:

Who was King Ahasuerus married to?

Why did he get angry at her?

What did he do about it?

Who raised Esther?

Who did the king choose to be the queen to replace Vashti?

How did Mordecai save the king's life?

What did Haman ask the king to do when Mordecai refused to bow to him?

Old Testament Saints and The Messiah

When Esther found what Haman had done, what did she do?

When the king found Mordecai was the man responsible for saving his life, what did he do for Mordecai?

What happened to Haman?

What happened to his ten sons?

Chapter Twenty:

How many children did Job have?

Was Job poor?

What happened to all his riches and children?

Why did the Lord allow this to happen?

Did Job's friends comfort him?

What did the Lord say when Job asked why these things were happening?

Was God angry at Job's friends?

What did God tell them to do?

Did God restore Job's riches and children?

How old was Job when he died?

Chapter Twenty-One:

What vision did Isaiah receive from God?

What did God say He would do for the people if they would repent?

Old Testament Saints and The Messiah

Did it frighten Isaiah when he had a vision of the Lord sitting on His throne?

What did Isaiah say?

What did the Seraphin do?

Why would Ahaz not ask a sign from the Lord?

Did the Lord give him a sign and what was the sign?

What did the Lord tell Isaiah would happen to Judah and Jerusalem in the last days?

What will happen to the people who transgressed against God?

What did the Lord reveal to Isaiah about the Messiah?

Chapter Twenty-Two:

God warned Jeremiah what would happen to Judah for their wickedness. What did He say would happen?

What did God say He would do if Judah and Israel would obey His word?

Did they do as God asked?

Did Jeremiah get married?

How did Jeremiah feel when the people would not do as he asked?

Old Testament Saints and The Messiah

Why did the Lord warn the people not to go to Egypt?

Who did Jeremiah say would take Judah captive?

What did Jeremiah say about the kings of Israel?

How long did the Lord make Judah serve the king of Babylon?

What did the Lord say would happen to Babylon at the end of the seventy years?

Chapter Twenty-Three:

Who took Ezekiel captive?

What did Ezekiel see when he received visions from God?

What did the Lord tell him to do?

What others did the Lord tell Ezekiel to prophesy against?

When God sent men throughout the city to ask the people questions, what did they ask them?

What happened to those who approved of the disgusting things happening in the city?

What happened when Ezekiel saw the valley of dry bones?

Did the Lord compare these dry bones to Israel?

What did the Lord tell Ezekiel would happen to Israel when they repented?

Chapter Twenty-Four:
Who seized Jerusalem and Jehoiakin, king of Judah?
What did he take from the Lord's house?
Who was taken captive by Nebuchadnezzar?
What new names were given to the captives?
Did they change their diets as the king requested?
Did they prove their diets were best?
What was Nebuchadnezzar's dream, and who interpreted it?
What happened to those who refused to bow down to the kings image?
What did the king see in the fiery furnace?
Who interpreted the kings second dream and what was the dream?
What happened at the party Belshazzar had?
Did Daniel tell them what this meant?
What happened to Belshazzar?
After the king issued a decree forbidding anyone from praying to anyone except him, what did he do to Daniel when he prayed to his God?

The king was relieved when he found Daniel safe. What did he do to the men who accused Daniel?

What vision did Daniel have of the end times?

Chapter Twenty-five:

How many of the minor prophrts can you name?

What are some of their accomplishments?

Chapter Twenty-Six:

Who was the mother of Jesus?

Who was His earthly father?

Where was Jesus born?

Was He born in a mansion?

Who followed the star to find Jesus?

What did they do when they saw Jesus?

When the wise men took a different direction home to avoid Herod, what did Herod do?

What was his reaction?

Where did the Lord tell Joseph to take his wife and child?

What reason did He give Joseph for doing this?

What did Herod do to the male children?

After Herod's death, where did the Lord tell Joseph to go?

Old Testament Saints and The Messiah

Who came preaching in the wilderness of Judea?

Who baptized Jesus?

What happened when Jesus came up out of the water?

What did God say about Jesus?

Where did Jesus go after He was baptized?

What happened to Him?

Did Jesus tell the people God's reason for sending Him to earth?

When Jesus went up on the mountain, what sermon did He preach?

Did Jesus perform any miracles? Name a few.

What activity did Jesus find when He went into the temple?

What did Jesus do?

What did Jesus say His house would be called?

What did Jesus tell His disciples would happen to Him?

Which disciple betrayed Jesus?

What did he receive for betraying Jesus?

What happened to the disciple who betrayed Jesus?

Who denied knowing Jesus three times?

Old Testament Saints and The Messiah

What prayer did Jesus pray before He was crucified?

Did His disciples watch when Jesus went to pray?

What did the false witness testify against Jesus?

What was Jesus' reaction when He was questioned?

Name some of the horrible things they did to Jesus before He was hung on the cross?

Was it a custom to release a prisoner at the time of the Passover?

Who did they release?

Where was Jesus crucified?

What did the people do while He hung on the cross?

Who was hung on crosses on each side of Jesus?

What happened when Jesus breathed His last breath?

Who asked for the body of Jesus?

Where did they bury Jesus?

How long was He in the tomb?

What happened when He arose from the tomb?

Did He appear to anyone after He came out of the tomb?

Old Testament Saints and The Messiah

What did Jesus tell His disciples to do just before He was taken up into heaven?

What did Jesus promise to those who overcome?

Did Jesus tell His disciples what would happen to the temple?

What happened to the temple?

Who did God send to witness the things that would happen in the end times?

What did Jesus tell the people would happen when the great tribulation comes?

After the great tribulation what did Jesus say would take place?

What will happen when the seventh seal is opened?

How many people will be killed?

What will happen when the angels sound their trumpets?

What happened when war broke out in heaven?

How long did God give the beast and false prophet authority to do the things they would do?

What will the beast and false prophet make the people do?

What will happen to the people who disobey them?

What will happen to the beast and false prophet?

Old Testament Saints and The Messiah

What will the angel do to the devil?

Will he ever be released?

Who will reign with Christ a thousand years?

Is this the first resurrection?

When will the rest of the dead live again?

What will happen after the thousand year reign?

What will happen to those not written in the Book of Life at the Great White Throne Judgment?

What will happen to the first heaven and earth?

What did John say would come down from heaven?

Printed in the United States
136428LV00002B/1/P